The Missing Pieces: A Compilation of Autism Stories

Edited by Polly Bouker & Teresa Johnson

The Missing Pieces: A Compilation of Autism Stories

© 2009

ISBN: 1448649854 and 9781448649853

Dedicated to the 1 in 150 children who have some form of autism, and the families who love them.

Contents

What is Autism?

Shannon Jones

What is autism? I'm not talking about the vague definitions like" a group of complex developmental brain disorders", or "a severe neurological developmental disability" or "a condition that interferes with a child's ability to communicate and interact socially". I'm asking, what does autism look like in your home or in your school? What, really, is autism?

In our home, autism is:

big, lost eyes in crowds and noisy spaces

laughing too loud in the library

needing to touch the china in Macy's over and over and over

asking,"Why do people have faces?" and "Will we ever run out of nature?"

an insatiable appetite for the same beans and rice for 10 years
straight

worrying about getting whiskers

knowing all the tunes and only a few random words to every song
ever heard

wishing a car could be a friend

wondering when dinosaurs will no longer be extinct

pacing in endless circles

kissing a pet ladybug

being tall on tiptoes

Persona

Kevin Sutherburg

"We are trapped in a maze of relationships,
Life goes on with or without you,
I swim in the sea of the unconscious,
I search for your heart, pursue my true self..."

-Shoji Meguro, "Pursuing My True Self"
Shin Megami Tensei: Persona 4 Original Soundtrack

I remember my first day of high school. That day, I walked in from the car lane, in awe of the fortress of education that stood before me, twisting my eyes this way and that. The crowd of students who jostled me somewhat as I walked in was daunting. Only one thought crossed my mind as I crossed the threshold:

Five hundred dollars says I don't last the week here.

I was nobody, and I knew it. I had barely managed to make it through middle school with my life, my sanity, and my soul. Being a low-end genius was bad enough: a 156 IQ and a penchant for

learning had already made me a target for the usual suspects, bullies and the like. To make matters worse, at the age of five, after a particularly rough first semester of kindergarten, I was diagnosed with Asperger's Syndrome. Asperger's was on the high end of the range of mental disorders known as the Autism Spectrum. From what I understood, autistic disorders inhibited social development, and depending on where you were on the spectrum, you could be anywhere from severely mentally disabled to near-genius level... as far as normal intelligence went.

So what did that mean for me? Well, being on the high end of the disorder meant that I was quite the pint-sized professor. I was usually the first to grasp new ideas in class, but every now and then I would fall behind due to lack of attentiveness. It wasn't that I couldn't do it... far from it. I already could, and it was through sheer boredom from being taught things I had already mastered that lead me to pursue my own interests in class. That was the first strike. The teachers and admins had already pegged me as a troubled child on that note alone. Throw in the fact that half my classmates despised me for (a being able to ace most tests without ever paying attention, and (b never really valuing socialization much (due to the disorder, but of course THEY didn't know that), not to mention my intolerance of being bullied and my habit of reacting violently to it, meant that I probably spent more time in the principal's office than in the classroom.

I had put up with it for 9 years. And things were steadily getting worse.

Probably the one thing I had going for me was that I had not attended the feeder school for Arlington High (where I was to attend high school). My parents had moved from our tiny residence in the city to a larger, more spacious home on the outskirts of the suburbs. This meant I was going to a different high school than my classmates from middle school, and I would be less well-known (or as I put it, less infamous) than if I had attended my former district's high school. Not to mention that Arlington had only been open for a year, and had a relatively small population given only freshman and sophomores were attending. (The juniors and seniors in Arlington's district were attending the high school in Millington that was where everyone went before AHS was constructed.) AHS also had a much better reputation than the high school I would've gone to had it not been for the move. Just that past year, a student had thrown a Molotov cocktail into the principal's office at that school, setting it ablaze. I knew my parents had decided to move for the one reason of keeping me away from THAT mess.

Nevertheless, I was still apprehensive.

My first class of the day was Honors Geometry. This was primarily a sophomore class, but thanks to my math skills I was able to receive credit for the freshman prerequisite, Algebra I, while in 8th grade. Hence, I was one of about 3 freshmen in a 25-or-so person class... and let me say, being surrounded by upperclassmen in your first hour of high school is nothing short of intimidating.

As class progressed, I worked in silence. Then, as we were packing up in anticipation of the bell, I felt a tap on my shoulder, and turned to see four or so sophomore girls looking at me. The one who had tapped me introduced herself and welcomed me to the class. The three others followed suit. When the bell rang, the five of us left together, having talked a bit about ourselves, and having felt a sense of comradeship between us.

Thus ended my first class at Arlington High.

As the year progressed, I began to realize some things. My first realization was that not everyone here was so bad. There were still hateful people and bullies, but they seemed to be fewer and far between. Despite occasional incidents with the aforementioned, I began to feel slightly more confident in myself... but still, I had very few friends, and was usually the one walking to class silently while others stopped to chat.

Out of all of the six classes I attended, my all-time favorite was Introduction to Theatre Arts I. I had ended up in the class because, while I had applied to Intro to Film and Video I as my Fine Arts requirement, the class had filled to maximum before I had registered, and I was forced to go with my second choice instead. However, my initial frustration at having been placed into a class I had not specified melted away during the first week or so. There was no other word to describe it: this class was FUN. The instructor was a long term substitute for the department head, who had unfortunately been hospitalized with cancer before the start of term. She started the class every day with some yoga exercises, and after we had all limbered up, we would act out scenes from different plays, then finish up the hour with some improvisation games or similar.

That was my first taste of the theatre arts, and it was sweet. After the department head returned from his sick leave, he took over the class and began auditions for the school play that year, *Curtain Going Up!*. I was tempted dearly to audition, but I felt that I would have trouble keeping up academically if I landed a role. Instead, I applied for backstage tech.

The one thing I noticed about being in a play, even as a techie, was the sense of comradeship between the cast and crew. The rehearsals and performance were some of the best times of my life, and when the show as over, I was thirsty for more. The following year I was no longer in an acting class, so when the time rolled around, I decided to audition... this time for an onstage role. Coincidentally, the play that year was probably the most clichéd high school Shakespearean production known to the modern world: *The Tragedy of Romeo and Juliet.*

The auditions were nerve wracking, and the week before the roles were announced was even worse. But my troubles were rewarded when, passing by the cast list posted outside of the drama department office, I noticed my name underneath the character role *Peter (Capulet servant).* My immediate whoop of triumph echoed all the way down the hallway, prompting quite a few teachers to stick their heads out the door and tell me to shut the heck up.

Soon after that, rehearsals started. Contrary to popular opinion, as I soon learned, there is more to acting then standing up onstage and saying a few lines. As our acting coach taught us, in order to express your character well, you had to move as the character would move, feel as the character would feel, think as the character would think. In short, you had to become that character. At this point I was a little nervous. How could I be comfortable being someone else when I had no confidence in being myself? If I couldn't even express myself in a social situation, how was it I was supposed to express the feelings of a completely different person?

But as it turned out, working onstage was easier than expected. I learned many things during the five months of rehearsal – how to summon the emotion needed for a particular scene on command, how to project my voice so that it carried to the far end of the theatre, how to move so as to not upstage my fellow actors, how to laugh, cry, crack jokes, and get angry. I learned the bare basics of swordplay (something I enjoyed immensely), and other things that would've been required of a man in 15th century Verona, Italy. And I learned even more offstage. I learned how to be a friend, how to help out without being helped in return, and what to talk about during the backstage luncheon. I noticed that, nobody though I might be in the hallways, my presence was valued in the theatre. Gradually I got to know my compatriots, and they I. For the first time, I had friends... and as weird as I thought I was, some of them were far weirder. But perhaps it was this that caused us to get along so well.

When it finally came time for performance, I was expecting to be targeted by various forms of produce, but to my surprise everyone who attended spoke of how well I did. Despite my doubts, I had played my character quite well. I had mastered the persona of Peter.

In the remaining two years of my high school career, the theatre played a special part in my life. Memorable times abounded. In one particular dual improvisation session, I was playing the part of a young child whilst one of my friends (a girl whom I happened to have a crush on at the time) played the part of my slightly psychotic mother. We had just finished an improvised argument and I had turned to run off, when she got caught up in the moment and karate chopped me in the shoulder with enough force to knock me to the ground, eliciting gales of laughter from everyone present, drama teacher included. Then there was my breathtaking dramatic interpretation of the final chapter of J.K. Rowling's novel *Harry Potter and the Deathly Hallows,* in which I acted both parts of the final battle scene between Harry and Voldemort. Then there were other school productions, such as the historical drama *The Miracle Worker* and the comedy/musical *Bye Bye Birdie.*

As my theatrical career and my academic career progressed, I noticed, for the first time in my life, that I was becoming slightly popular. Most everyone at school knew my name, and at lunch, rather than sitting alone, I would sit with people from the theatre classes, where we would discuss different productions from around town. Some of my fondest memories would come from hanging out with "the drama crew", whether it was during class, at lunch, or backstage on our latest production.

To this day, I consider my involvement in theatre a key component in my social "awakening", per se. My life, it seems, is not without a sense of irony. In theatre, you strive to become someone else. You take the persona of someone who lived in the distant past, or on another continent, or even someone who never lived at all save on the pages of a script. You take these many different personas and you wear them like a mask onstage, to the entertainment of the audience. But maybe – just maybe – by being an actor and wearing the personas of many different people, I was able to finally don the most challenging persona of all: myself.

Our Mountain

Polly Bouker

For those of the Christian tradition, we think of church as a place built on the teachings of Jesus Christ, and a place where you can feel the most safe and accepted. Yeah, right.

Churches are often confined places where the seats or pews are close together. The services have an order to them, which often includes times of quiet prayer and teaching. Sitting close to other people during a quiet service can seem like climbing Mt. Everest for a family with a child who has autism.

At one church, my children and I would grab the last pew where we would stay during the music and would then retreat to the church foyer to listen to the pastor's sermon over speakers, or leave altogether. We didn't want to disturb others who were not aware of *why* Jon was so rambunctious and noisy, and *why* he didn't go to Sunday school with the other children. After several years of going there, people still welcomed us as visitors.

Another time during a Bible study with a small group of adults (and Jon, of course, since he is *always* with us), one of the other adults was talking and used the saying "witch with a B" to indicate how a familiar curse word had been used by someone in their life. Jon, who had been in his own world drawing, sat straight up and proudly yelled out, "bitch" with a huge smile on his face. He was so proud of figuring out the word, while we were so mortified!

Another memorable time was on an Easter Sunday when my husband was unable to join the children and me at church. After the passion play, my 8 yr old daughter, Hannah, decided to go to the front of the church to show that she had decided to accept Jesus as her savior. She was afraid to go alone and wanted me to go with her. Without Larry there, that meant that Jon would have to join us – horror of horrors! The pastor had a microphone in his hand and stretched it out to Hannah to ask her name, when Jon grabbed it and blurted into it, "I'm a scientist." Hannah and I nearly died right on the spot.

We still do our best to go to church and to bring our children up in our Christian tradition, but it is still difficult. Even at age 10, Jon cannot participate in children's church with the "typical" children because he becomes too excited and disruptive. He still cannot sit quietly with us and often has to be taken in and out during the service, and sometimes his behavior prevents us from going at all.

He is a person who needs the positive teachings of Jesus Christ and the fellowship and social experiences that a church can bring. We are a family that needs to be recharged by being around other people of our same faith. But, because his progress is slow, and most people don't understand or have experience with the autistic mind, church continues to be the Mt. Everest of our lives.

Simple Words
Sonya Bell

My son has autism and was nonverbal for almost three years. His first words were, "I want some toast." I was so excited. Then later on that day he said, "I want sausage." I could not be restrained from calling our family and friends.

That was a very happy day.

He's Come So Far

Teresa Johnson

Today was a remarkable day. Today, during our Fall Break from school, Rusty had an MRI and an EEG to determine if he is having seizures. 1 in 4 adolescents with autism have seizures show up at this time in their lives. While we have not seen anything recently, we have been concerned about a few things and want to rule out any possibility that something may be wrong.

I got up this morning, almost dreading the day ahead. 4 years ago, we tried to have an MRI performed before putting Rusty on a drug for aggression. It was part of a research study at the Medical College of Georgia. That one just didn't work out. Too loud, too long, too close quarters, just too much.

Today, we made our trek to Athens, first to the University of Georgia to pick up an autographed football from Coach Mark Richt to be part of our annual raffle at Jingle Jog for Autism and raise money for our summer camp. We had no idea that the building we would walk into would be like a museum! We didn't have long to stay, but walked around and promised to return. The receptionist told us of some other things available and said to call her and she would set up something with some of the other children who wanted to join us. What a great place UGA is!

After a quick drive-thru Chick-fi-A, we entered the Diagnostics Center. The wait was short, and during that time, I was explaining what was to come, to prepare Rusty for this experience. I mentioned that this was going to be loud, and last about an hour. I also mentioned that this would be done with and without contrast, meaning he would need a shot. I could see the respirations pick up, needles are not a friend to Rusty. He said 'NO' and I said, 'ok, lets just get the first part done'. And he did great. Did not move an inch during the entire scan, was just perfect.

We had about an hour down time before the EEG, so we visited a Halloween store just down the street. With just 5 days until the ghostly holiday, which included a trip to my sister, Sharon's, we decided to purchase a costume to wear. Rusty had chosen a wild punk clown mask at another store a few weeks ago, but wanted to get an outfit to go with it. He selected a blind referee, something that will be hilarious since the Georgia-Florida game will be this Sat, a favorite of ours. I selected a Tavern Wench and got John a pirate hat and eye patch with earring. I am sure we'll be the life of the party!

Then came the EEG. Again the wait was short, and we entered a room with a queen size bed. Wow, I thought, I could take a nap on that! The technician had him lay with his head on an incline at the end of the bed, proped by a towel as a pillow. It took nearly 45 minutes for the electrodes to be applied to his head. I kept waiting for him to jump up, pull them off and run out the door. This has happened at various times in the past, including pulling an IV out of his hand after outpatient dental surgery. He didn't move. In fact, he didn't move or say a word at either of these appointments, another clear indication to those working on him that he did in fact have autism, even though he looks so normal.

At the conclusion, he finally asked "are we done?" as he was a bit tired of the wires hanging from his head. As the technician was removing them, he touched the gooey stuff used to adhere them to his head. In the past, he would have freaked out. He just said "can you get this stuff off my ear?" WOW, what a difference.

We left and I immediately drove him back to Chick-fil-A and rewarded him with 2 brownies for the effort. He earned it today. My fears were unfounded, but more importantly, God answers prayer. As I do each day, I ask for God's hand to be upon him and today was just an amazing day.

Acceptance

Sharon Jones

It was a cool, crisp autumn evening when my son Kyle and I set out to attend a Friday night high school football game. My husband was out of town so we decided to go support my friend's daughter who was marching in the band at her school. Just as we all got settled in the stands Kyle decided it would be a good time for a restroom break. We climbed down the bleachers and all the way across the track to the restrooms that were located at the high school. There were many people coming and going as it is at most high school football stadiums this time of year. Students are excited to socialize with their friends and support their team.

As we approached the restrooms, that is when it hit me – my husband was not there to take Kyle to the men's restroom. Kyle is 14 years old and he has autism with a moderate intellectual disability and if you didn't know, men's restrooms are filled with "social land mines" for children on the autism spectrum. My husband and I have gone to great lengths to teach Kyle proper restroom etiquette – "Wait your turn for a urinal" (there is no sharing), "don't stand right next to someone if there is an empty urinal across the room," "face forward," "hands to yourself," etc. My gut reaction was to take him into the girl's restroom like I used to do when he was young, but there were teenage girls everywhere. Kyle is 14 but he is 6' tall and 200 pounds and I didn't want to traumatize anyone. By this time adrenaline was coursing through my body and I started in on Kyle with a quick review of the "rules" of the restroom. I had to let him go alone into the "social land mine" with no support. Where is a paraprofessional when you need one? Surely he could do this alone – what could possibly go wrong?

As Kyle entered the restroom I stood outside the doorway still yelling out helpful tips – "You may have to wait in line," "wash your hands," but nothing me, my husband or teachers had ever taught Kyle could prepare him for what was to come. Standing at the mirror in the hallway was a young man who had spray painted his almost naked body sparkly blue and gold. He was adjusting his metallic gold wig just as Kyle got near. It was then that time shifted into slow motion, my mind raced forward to what was about to happen. Kyle approached the young man and proceeded to touch him from his metallic gold wig all over his shiny painted body. Now if you stop and think about it Kyle just did what most of us would have wanted to do. The student truly looked like something from outer space. Of course it is socially inappropriate to touch a stranger in this manner, right?

I knew Kyle was going to touch this student and then he was going to get the beating of his life. Teenage boys would not put up with another boy touching them like Kyle did. As I stood in the doorway I began screeching at Kyle in that "mommy voice" I had developed to make him stop in his tracks. "Stop it. Don't touch him" I yelled as I debated running into the restroom to intervene. The young man stood there, adjusted his wig and headed to the exit. Apologies started flowing from my mouth as I tried to explain why Kyle has, with no remorse or understanding of the potential ramifications, fondled his shiny body. The student looked at me and said, "It's no problem, I totally understand. He's fine – really ma'am, its okay."

After the boy walked away it came to me. Kyle did not get punched in the face that day because this student had seen "my child" before. Maybe autistic children had been in his homeroom, lunch room, PE class, or hopefully in his academic classes at school. Somewhere along the way this typical boy had been in contact with children like Kyle and he got t - tolerance and acceptance for each other. Kyle isn't all that different than other children, he is a person first, before any of his many labels.

Tears still come to my eyes each time I tell this story. I thank the educators, parents and people in our communities who include children like Kyle – if not for him for all the other kids who may get to know Kyle and discover his worth. I can only hope that the shiny boy with that enthusiastic school spirit grows up to teach his family about the Kyle's of the world. Maybe he will be a leader in his community, a policy maker and pass along his understanding and compassion for our kids.

Thank You
Melissa Line

For Christmas, my Grandmother gave Mitchell a T-Rex that you assemble and then use a small controller to make the T-Rex come to life. He roars and moves his head and tail. It is a really fun toy!

At breakfast on the morning after Christmas, I asked the kids to tell me about their favorite Christmas present. In spite of the fact that John and I spent approximately 49 man-hours tracking down the odd assortment of items that he requested from Santa, including PVC pipes and mirrors to make a periscope, Mitchell's favorite gift of Christmas 2008 was the T-Rex. The entire model was completely assembled by 9 pm, and the new companion sits in a place of honor at the highest point of the lego table in his bedroom. Every night that I read the bedtime story, Mitchell looks down from the top bunk and says: "Push the button on my T-Rex" before he can go to sleep.

Recently when John had to work, the kids and I packed a picnic lunch and planned to take advantage of the beautiful weather.

When I told them we were going to Yahoola Creek Reservoir, Mitchell asked if he could bring an "invention" he had made earlier in the morning. The newest contraption was a "grabber" that used two small pieces of rope and the head of the T-Rex. By pulling both ropes at the same time, the T-Rex would open its jaws. Then, Mitchell would clamp the head of the T-Rex over a household object (say, a paint can) and lift it in the air. He was pretty excited about the invention, so I agreed to let him bring it along.

While Georgia, Samuel and I were eating our lunch, Mitchell ran down to the edge of the water and started "casting" the head of his T-Rex into the water. When I walked down to ask him what he was doing, he informed me that he was "fishing" with his new invention. No sooner had I started up the bank when I heard a very loud cry of despair. Sadly, the fishing contraption had failed and the head of the beloved T-Rex floated away in the dark, muddy water.

Mitchell was so sad he couldn't eat his picnic lunch. The lunch included all of his favorites - peanut butter and jelly sandwich, funyons, an orange drink and his all time favorite dessert - a chocolate Hershey's candy bar! Frustrated and anxious, he hunted for a stick long enough to reach the floating head of the T-Rex. He found a piece of rope on the boat dock and tied two very long sticks together, convinced that he could reach the T-Rex.

This rescue attempt went on for what seemed like hours. The green plastic head bobbed in the water and every stick that he flung towards it only served to push it out deeper.

Now, in order to appreciate the next part of this story, you have to understand that for the past year there has been an invisible wall between Mitchell and myself. When I first met John's kids, I knew I could win Georgia over. I had no worries about befriending a young teenage girl because I have (thanks to my Amanda) plenty of experience in breaking the ice. I was equally confident about blending in with Samuel because, even though he is stubborn and strong-willed, he longs for rules and boundaries. Mitchell has been my biggest challenge, partly due to his autism, but also due to his undying devotion to his biological mom. For the first half of 2008, Mitchell was convinced that any kindness shown toward me was a betrayal of his mother.

So, there we stood on the bank of Yahoola Creek Reservoir, a beautiful sun shining overhead, and I knew what had to be done. Rolling my jeans up to my knees, I kicked off my shoes and socks, and waded out into the water. Although it was a warm 65 degrees outside, the lake wasn't aware of the change in weather. I felt like I was walking through a brown slushie frozen drink, with God-only-knows floating around me. When the water was just under my belt line, I reached the head of Mitchell's T-Rex and proudly thrust it into the air. On the boat dock, Mitchell cheered and jumped up and down.

I wasn't expecting a great show of thanks, but as I unrolled my sopping wet jeans, Mitchell threw his arms around me in a loving embrace. "Thank you, Melissa!" he beamed.

"You're welcome, honey," I told him, hobbling toward my shoes and socks and shivering from the cold. I used the picnic blanket to dry off my legs as Mitchell joined his brother and sister in eating their lunches. While I was loading the wet picnic blanket into the back of my jeep, Mitchell came around and stood beside me. After another long hug, he smiled. "Thank you for saving my T-Rex," he said, and lovingly handed me his Hershey bar as a reward.

"My child has what? What does that mean?"

Teresa Johnson

That was the response of a young mother upon learning her child had just been given the "Big A" diagnosis. "Autism."   Very little information about autism was available. The doctor recommended speech therapy, occupational therapy, vision therapy, social skills therapy. There were other challenges besides autism. "Where do you get these therapies, who pays for them, how am I going to manage my work schedule, and what about my other child?" And so life with a child on the autism spectrum began.   And the thoughts and actions of this mother were like a runaway train!

"He is just 4 years old and his behaviors are down right embarrassing. Why does he have to act like that? Nothing seems to work to get his attention. Get up off the dirty floor at Wal-mart! Please stop screaming! People are staring"; someone yells "isn't that boy too big to be acting like that?" "Shut up and mind your own business" she says in her head, while trying to regain her composure, grab up her screaming child, and leave an hour's worth of shopping sitting in the checkout lane because it was all she could do. He falls asleep on the way home. An average day is getting up at 7, making breakfast, getting the oldest child out to board the school bus (Is he just in 1st grade? He seems to have grown up over night!) then the schedule of therapies, all in Atlanta and a full day of driving, waiting, therapy, getting home in time for the oldest son to get off the bus, make dinner, manage behavior meltdowns, clean up messes, do laundry, oh, and homework. Then collapse into bed.

"Why did this have to happen to me?" She asks this over and over again for years. "Where do I turn to for help?" The pediatrician said "go to your school and they will provide speech therapy". After an assessment, she learns that he is Significantly Developmentally Delayed. That's what opened this Pandora's Box that led to the "Autism" diagnosis by a private neuropsychologist. The pediatrician suspected as much. She and her husband attend conferences in Atlanta and Birmingham trying to learn more. The Internet is her library as she reads for hours. What happens when he goes to school?

He started as a preschooler in the special needs classroom with an SDD eligibility. At the conference, she hears things she has never heard! "What are parental rights? What is IDEA? What are all those letters and what do they mean? IEP, IDEA, BIP, FBA, OT, SLP, PT, VT, and the list goes on and on. What do you mean the school is supposed to offer these services since my child has a diagnosis of autism? Why are they withholding information and special education from my child? What is a 504, what is an IEP? I am angry and not going to take it anymore! Tell me about Due Process. I am calling in a complaint to the State Dept of Education! I have talked to Nancy O'Hara in the complaint department, you're in trouble now!! I am going to file a court order if you don't get this straight. Do I have to tell you how to do your job? I may as well home school so my child gets the therapies he needs, he sure isn't getting them at school. I can teach him better than you, you don't care about him and don't know how to deal with a child who has autism in your classroom. Wait, I need an advocate, where do I find one? You mean I have to pay for that too? When do the costs go down? I can't take him out of school for therapy, so I guess he will have to give up therapy. Tell me again why he only gets 30 minutes of OT a MONTH when he has a Written Expression disability???? Now he is in High School and still can't write. You don't know our history! What do you mean his case manager isn't his teacher? You mean even if he passes the classes, he may not graduate? He has to do what to earn a diploma? What is GHSGT? You mean he has to WRITE a paper to graduate? He still has Written Expression!!"

As you can guess, this mom is me and these are the many thoughts I have gone through with 14 years of public schooling in Walton County after learning my son was delayed. And while it seems an exaggeration, these thoughts are an accurate display of the roller coaster ride of thoughts and emotions that I have felt since hearing the words "your son has autism". It affects every member of my family both positively and negatively. And we are not alone. Parents across Walton County have shared similar thoughts, fears, and anxiety over what their child's future will look like if they don't see progress in their goals or placement during the year. I now stop screaming and offer support to the best of my ability as a parent mentor.

BFF

Sonya Bell

As a parent, you always worry about your kids. When they have special needs, you tend to worry more. I have always prayed that Isaiah would have a bff (best friend forever). Although, I don't know if they will be friends forever, I do know that for the past two years his best friend has been Darius. To see them play and laugh together just warms my heart.

Darius does not see autism in Isaiah, but instead he sees his bff! This is evident when he proudly tells everyone that his best friend is Isaiah.

Love

Krystal Wales

My sister Madison has the most amazing blue green eyes like no one has ever seen. She has the cutest little face with her long eyelashes and freckles dusted under her eyes and across her nose. She is the sweetest, most adorable, and shy little kid but make her angry and she can be as ill as a hornet.

She has a neurobiological disorder called autism.

She loves to steal my things - especially my videotapes and my stuffed animals. She really loves my tiger stuffed animal that my step dad won for me at the Gwinnett County Fair. She loves to wear jewelry like rings and necklaces. She has her ears pierced but do not let her know you are going to change the pair she has in unless you have something to bribe her with. She is my silly, sweet sister. I love her with all my heart and without her I probably would have died.

Play With Me

Judith Labrozzi

Grandpa and Jon have a unique relationship - a result of Grandpa's refusal to accept that there is anything wrong with Jon that can't be cured by "outgrowing" it. Because of this attitude, Grandpa doesn't feel it necessary to interact differently with Jon. Their best moments are when Jon wants Grandpa to "play" a computer game with him.

Grandpa has learned that he won't actually get to play (heaven forbid) but that he is expected to sit next to Jon and watch. If he should dare to touch the mouse, Jon carefully takes Grandpa's hand and moves it away. Recently Jon cried because Grandpa couldn't sit and play with him. When reminded that he never allowed Grandpa to play anyway, Jon's response was "I was going to let him play this time".

Of Lead and Angels

Christine Nessel

Ethan was diagnosed with Lead Poisoning when he was about 3 ½ years old. We had just relocated for work and my job came with a beautiful old Victorian home as part of my package. He had been in the Birth to Three Program and had been classified as having Pervasive Developmental Disorder, Not Otherwise Specified (PDD-NOS). This is a nice way of saying your child has a problem, but we don't know what it is. He was sent to all sorts of specialists by his pediatricians. Not one of them thought he was autistic. He didn't fit the stereotype because he was outgoing and craved physical touch. He was too happy of a child to be autistic, even though he had little to no eye contact, toe-walked, and had lost all language.

My mother-in-law heard a story about mercury poisoning and mentioned to us that we should have Ethan tested for heavy metal poisoning. When we asked his pediatrician what she thought she dismissed the idea and sent us to a pediatric geneticist (an appointment we had to wait four months to get yet a short wait in the grand scheme of scheduling appointments with pediatric specialists).

By this time Ethan had begun preschool with a wonderful teacher in a fairly good school, but every other day we were getting calls from the school nurse that he was having "bowel issue," aka explosive diarrhea. We'd go pick him up from school, get him home and he would be fine for a day or two. Then we would get another call from the school nurse. We were on a first name basis with her and one day she casually asked if Ethan had ever been tested for lead.

School nurses can often be portrayed as nurses who couldn't cut it in a real nursing job. Like people with autism, school nurses fall into stereotypes. But I will forever be grateful for this one because she saved his life.

When we told her that his doctor had dismissed the idea of the $8 blood test for lead and was sending us to a pediatric geneticist whose bill was considerably larger, she told us that she would request the test from the doctor. The next Monday I took him for his first of many blood tests and by Wednesday we were driving him to the hospital. It was the week before Thanksgiving.

Often times when a person goes through a particularly painful time someone offers those "comforting" words: one day you'll look back on all this and laugh. Four years later and I can honestly say I have yet to look back and laugh at what happened after his diagnosis.

Ethan and his dad spent two nights in the hospital while I stayed with our daughter in our lead infested house. The department of health inspected our beautiful old home and clearly stated that child welfare would take Ethan from us if we let him back into the house before work was done and they had cleared it. From there we moved into a hotel that specializes in long-term stays. For 41 nights, in the middle of winter, we stayed in a two bedroom suite with a kitchenette and the dog, only a 45 minute drive from home and work. The best thing I can say about that was they had an indoor heated pool and they let our daughter, Rachel, put the Christmas ornament she made at school on the hotel's tree in the lobby.

From the hotel we moved into a 2 bedroom apartment with the dog and two cats. There we stayed for 4 more months while all the woodwork in our home was scraped and covered in special chemicals, our kitchen was gutted and remodeled, all our windows were replaced, our garage was re-sided, and half our yard was dug out to remove the lead. I now know where the term, "get the lead out" comes from.

Lead levels are measured two ways: blood level (the level of lead in the blood system) and body burden level (the level of lead in soft tissues, organs, and bones), both should be zero. Ethan's blood level was in the 60's. People with blood lead levels in the 70's suffer from brain damage and death. Ethan's body burden was in the 500's. We fired our pediatrician and found a new one. The first thing the new doctor said to us was, "I don't know anything about lead poisoning, so I'm going to send you to the experts."

The experts were the people at the Lead Clinic at Yale New Haven Hospital in Connecticut. It was there we met Judy, another nurse who has helped save Ethan's life in many ways. Our new pediatrician referred us to a pediatric psychiatrist, but we would have to wait for over a year for that appointment. In conversations with Judy we mentioned our frustration about having to wait to see the new specialist. "We have someone here who could see him", she told us and at the next appointment Dr. S. was in the room asking us all sorts of questions about Ethan.

Within a few weeks we were sitting in her office hearing the words: severe autism. I think we knew somewhere deep down that was what we were going to hear. It was almost a relief to have that word attached to our son, to understand why he did what he did and why he was the way he was.

We will never know what kind of impact the lead has had on Ethan, but we do know that his autism played a role in him getting the lead poisoning. Lead paint tastes sweet. The ironic flip side to this is that the treatment for heavy metal poisoning (chelation) smells like a cross between rotten eggs and baby poop. Because Ethan loves to eat and still puts everything in his mouth like a toddler it didn't take much for him to develop the repetitive habit of eating lead paint. Because he was autistic he was at a high risk for ingesting lead infected stuff.

My mother believes that Ethan has a guardian angel. The lead was just one of many close calls we've had, although perhaps the worst. I think she is right. I've seen the angels several times in the forms of doctors and nurses and teachers and regular ordinary people who find ways to intercede on his behalf, and I am grateful.

Never Give Up

Teresa Johnson

Today I celebrate a success I have spent months worrying over. I celebrate the uniqueness of my child, and the promise for his future. Today, I take a deep breath and ask myself, "why do you stress out so much!"

Today, the results for the Georgia High School Graduation Tests came in. For those who do not have children in high school, let me explain. In GA, students who wish to obtain a Regular Education diploma MUST pass 5 content areas in Math, Social Studies, Science, Language Arts and Writing. This is in addition to the rigorous courses of high school in the multi content areas that would lead to college and earning of Carnegie credits in each course to obtain a regular education as opposed to a special education diploma.

Today, Rusty succeeded in passing the Math and Social Studies portions of this test. It is a major accomplishment. Science,

Language Arts and Writing remain a challenge, but I feel more hope today than I have felt in months. Maybe a Regular Diploma is now within his reach. Maybe in May 2010, he can don his cap and gown and walk across the stage at Loganville High School and receive what we all hope for in our children: Completion and success in his education. He will have 4 more opportunities to pass these 3 tests in the next year. We hope it only takes 1!

My word of encouragement to you today is simply this.... DO NOT GIVE UP ON YOUR CHILD! You never know what they are capable of and how they will surprise you! Whether your child can attain the Regular or a Special Ed diploma, it is about them and their successes, not ours! Find the incentive that works to motivate your child, no matter what it takes! Rusty reminded me that I owed him $25 for passing each portion of this test, a small incentive to complete the test fully. It will be a pleasure to give him $50. And I look forward to spending $75 more when he passes the remaining 3!

We are not out of the woods, but we can see the light at the end of the tunnel and hope abounds. Keep your eyes forward, encourage your child every step of the way! Celebrate the small things! I am one very happy mom tonight!

Be strong and courageous. Do not be afraid: do not be discouraged, for God is with you wherever you go.   Joshua 1:9

PS. He passed the Lang Arts on the 2nd attempt, now to master Science and Writing!

Seeing

Sonya Bell

When my seven year old got his glasses, he walked outside and said, "Wow I can see the leaves!"

I Love You With Blueberry Muffins

Shannon Johnson

My son is 12 years old. He has recently told me that he is done with kisses. I'm not allowed to even pucker my lips within 20 feet of him. Hugs are occassional and always on his terms. So, I'm relearning how to say I love you to this boy/adolescent. Perhaps something fresh from the oven might help him feel loved and valued:

I Love You With Blueberry Muffins by Mom

I love you with blueberry muffins
All sugar and flour and eggs
Rounded tops with golden peaks
Twelve to a recipe
Tucked into tupperware.

I love you at 400 degrees fahrenheit
Perfectly moist in the center
Firm bottom and edges
Easily removed from the tin

Releasing steam on a silver rack.

I love you with a blue mouthful
A squished berry underfoot
Stained fingers and teeth
And "just one more, please"
Saving some for another day.

My Little Sunshine
Deborah Turk

Moriah, my 10 year old daughter who has autism, is considered nonverbal because she has very little words. Her name means mountain of light, so you may ask why I called her my little sunshine. It's because when I am feeling gloomy she comes along with a big smile on her face and looks at me. It brings a burst of sunshine on a cloudy day.

Anniversary

Margaret Spielman

If I asked you where you were on September 11, 2001, I am sure you could all remember EXACTLY what you were doing. However, if I asked you where you were on February 17, 1996 at 6:30pm, I am sure most of you wouldn't remember. For me that was the day I got the call that my son had a disability. Tomorrow is our 13-year anniversary of his diagnosis. I find it strange to even think about it because usually it's not really on my mind. This year is different.

Maybe it's because I am a new mom and I worry about how to raise a typical child, or maybe it's because I had to revisit those memories today. As I sit here, I look back at the girl I was and now the woman he has helped me to become. I look back at all the opportunities that have been afforded to me because of his disability and the great strides he has made not because I am his mother, but because of the great team of teachers, doctors, friends, family and community partners that joined me in deciding that pretty good wasn't enough for him. Everyone has played a part in his success.

They have taken the attitude that failure is not an option and that if we expect greatness, he will most certainly give it.

When asked to describe him today I said he is the child that has the faith of a mustard seed, the courage of a lion, and an unconditional love for ALL people. Is he perfect? No. Difficult at times? Yes. Worth it? Definitely!

So as I awaken in the morning, I will remember that 13 years ago God revealed to me through my son the beginning of the plans for me that he spoke about in Jeremiah. I will remember that in my brokenness he was able to bring forth in me courage, faith, determination, compassion and love. I will give thanks for all that he has done in Hunter's and my life and for what he has promised to do.

Last but not least, I will take a moment to give thanks and love to my child for never letting me stay at the pity party too long, for reminding me that life is hard but giving up is not an option, and that any limitations that are put on him were not set by him but by others who saw his disability as a weakness. I will thank him for the joy, unconditional love, courage, determination, faith, compassion and patience that he freely gives to ALL with whom he comes in contact and that he graciously gives to me.

Years ago when I worked at a bank, I would go to the top floor of the parking deck and sit in a corner to eat my lunch. It was quiet there and I could relax and just enjoy the weather without having to entertain anyone. One day while eating I dropped a piece of a crunchy Cheeto on the ground beside me. I went about eating my lunch and decided to pick it up after I was finished. However, there was an ant that had different plans. I sat there and watched as a small ant came out of a tiny crack in the concrete and picked up that piece of Cheeto. The Cheeto was significantly larger than the ant, but he picked it up and began to take it back to his home.

As he arrived at the entrance he found that the Cheeto was slightly larger than the crack, so he began to work with it. He moved the Cheeto around to different angles until he finally got it in. I thought this was amazing so I told one of my friends. I then asked this question, "How can an itty bitty ant pick up a big piece of Cheeto?" Expecting to hear the scientific explanation, I waited. He replied, "No one ever told him he couldn't!" I thought about what he said and I knew he was right! There was no one there who said, "Oh, you are too small; you can't do that!" or "You need to just leave that there and let the bigger, more experienced ants get it!" He did it because failure was not an option. He did it because he believed that greatness comes when you stop saying that things are impossible and start saying, I'm Possible!

But, what did you really mean?
Polly Bouker

While driving in the car with my 10 yr old son, Jon, I was lecturing him about his behavior and the fact that I was so disappointed that he had lied to me. After my lengthy lecture while he stared into space, he turned to me and asked, "Did you really fall off of a turnip truck?"

Teresa Johnson

Rusty is an avid fan of brownies. I think he dreams in chocolate. One day, I was called to come pick him up from school because of his behaviors and I was quite frustrated with him about it. On the ride home, I made the statement "you had better get your act together, because you aren't earning any brownie points with me!" He looked wide-eyed at me and asked, "You made brownies?" It was priceless!

What's That Shiny Red Thing?

Christine Nessel

Many children with autism like to push, pull, flip, tap, and bang on all sorts of things and Ethan is no exception.

My husband decided that we should take a road trip one day and visit a friend who lived 3 hours away. We were going to meet in the middle, but traffic and weather made the journey much longer than it should have been and left us with a very small amount of time to visit with our friend. Instead of going to our original meeting spot we chose to meet at a rest stop on the highway where we took turns occupying Ethan by walking him around and around the building and feeding him red licorice as we visited with each other.

By the time we said goodbye it was dinnertime. Ethan and his older sister, Rachel, were both complaining that they wanted to eat, but none of us wanted to stay where we were. So we climbed into the car and headed back towards home. Eventually we picked another rest stop and while their dad took the two kids inside for the potty and food I went to get gas in the car.

Once the tank was full I headed into the building through a mini mart attached to the gas station and the rest stop and decided it made sense to buy some quick snacks and drinks for the rest of the ride home. Nothing calms Ethan down the way food does.

When I showed my daughter the snack I had picked out for her she wasn't happy about it and complained until I agreed to let her pick out something else and exchange it as we were leaving. In the middle of the transaction, my husband, who had been cleaning up the mess of nuggets and French fries that Ethan had left back in the restaurant walked by and relieved me of the kids. He had Rachel out the door, but for some reason, still unbeknownst to me, stopped at the door with Ethan right next to the fire alarm.

I saw it happen a second too late. I was holding out my hand for the change from the candy on the counter when the alarm started flashing and wailing. That "oh my God" look spread across my husband's face and the cashier announced, "That's it. Everybody out."

Assuring her that my son had pulled the alarm and there was no fire, I grabbed the change and candy while thanking her and apologizing all in one breath as my husband quickly herded the children towards the car. Outside the door I realized that the alarms were going off throughout the gas station, the mini mart, and the main part of the rest stop building. I yelled: "Let's get the you-know-what out of here!"

It wasn't until we were several miles away that we started laughing.

About a week later my husband had to go away for a week on business and I had the task of taking Ethan to the hospital for dental surgery. Rachel stayed with a friend, and Ethan's favorite person, Grandmom, came along with me to help out.

Because Ethan couldn't do his favorite thing in the whole world ,which is eating or drinking, we let him walk the pre-op floor as we waited for the anesthesiologist and dentist to come do their thing before taking him in for surgery.

We thought we were clever by standing at opposite ends of the hall in the pre-op area. The staff kept telling us how cute he was with his red hair and too long hospital pants as he walked back and forth, back and forth, occasionally breaking into a run or stopping to hold our hands and jump up and down.

But, there was the fire alarm all bright and red and shiny and no where near where Mommy or Grandmom was standing.

The alarm went off just as the dentist walked through the doors and asked if the all the ruckus was because she was in the building. Another doctor explained to her with a wink and a smile that we had a trouble-maker and he was going to be keeping an eye on him.

Needless to say, we now watch out for fire alarms when we have Ethan in public.

Big Sister

Christine Nessel

The best advice I ever received about parenting came from a college friend when I was pregnant with Ethan. She had just had her second child and told me that she and her husband had made a concerted effort to include their son in their second pregnancy. They never referred to the baby in her belly as anything but "our baby." They talked to him about names and all the things that would happen when his sister was born. It meant that he, as the big brother, had a stake in this new person who would be arriving into their lives.

So we did the same thing with Rachel. She would rub, pat, kiss and talk to her baby brother in my belly. He was hers as much as he was our child. I'll never forget bringing him home and telling her I needed to change his diaper. She went running on her almost three year old legs to the front door then dragged the stuffed diaper bag into the bedroom in order to help.

There are days that we wonder how we would survive without her and her vigilant care of her brother. We often refer to her as the third parent and there are times I have to remind her that I am actually his mommy, not her.

I remember reading an article about siblings of children with autism. The article talked about how children who had brothers or sisters with disabilities often became highly caring and compassionate adults, but the same wasn't necessarily true for siblings of autistic people. Because it's difficult for many people with autism to express themselves or to tolerate physical touch,they don't give the same kind of feedback to their siblings the way a child with another disability might.

The article terrified me as it went on to describe unhealthy levels of stress for siblings of autistic persons. I can deal with the unfairness of my own stress as a mom to a special needs child (well, most of the time at least), but this really hurt my heart as a mom.

Rachel endures a great level of unfairness because of her brother's condition, but she also embraces being his big sister. She hates it that there are things he can't do and hates it that there are things we can't do as a family because of his autism. She despises the fact that sometimes there are things we don't always do simply because of the time and effort it takes to do them, such as going out to dinner as a family which can be a complete disaster, spending the day at the beach which becomes an exercise in futility because he will run and eat sand, or not taking a trip to visit friends because we are afraid that their home won't be Ethan-proofed enough.

This past Christmas, Rachel and I wrote a letter to Santa to leave with his cookies. What she wanted more than anything else was for her non-verbal brother to be able to say her name and tell her that he loved her. I have no doubt that Ethan loves his sister. She is his best friend, his best teacher, and his best advocate. This is what Santa told her in his reply: "I know for a fact" he wrote, "that Ethan loves you very much and that he will find all sorts of ways to tell you that." The joy on her face when she read those words was a balm for my soul.

At 10 years old Rachel has three ambitions in life. Ask her what she wants to be when she grows up and she will tell you, "An artist, or a teacher for children with autism, or a rock star." While her dad and I take pride in the fact that she wants to teach children just like her brother we also secretly hope that she will become the rock star. But we also have other dreams for her: to be happy and healthy, compassionate and independent, to love and be loved.

And, we know that whatever her achievements are in life that she will always be the most amazing big sister to her sweet brother.

A Higher Purpose
Rhonda Hammons

Kensi had her 1st MRI this morning. They gave her an oral medication to relax her so they could put the IV in for the full sedation. After the medicine kicked in, Kensi began to get drowsy and rested without saying a word for about 25 minutes. Then, the anesthesiologist came in and injected the stronger IV anesthesia.

Just as she injected the stronger medication, even with Kensi's language delays, she said the most incredible words: "I have a higher purpose," and then she fell asleep. This was from a 4 1/2 year old with autism who can't yet put 4 words together in the right order to make a coherent sentence.

She never ceases to amaze me and she always proves to me that you absolutely cannot underestimate a person who has autism. To me, this is just proof from God that the sky is the limit for our kids. They all have a higher purpose.

How One Little Girl Changed The World By Changing Her Mom and Transforming Her Community

Melinda Smith - Pace

She is my inspiration, my Francie. Francie has autism but that does not define her in any way. She is the most amazing little girl I have met. Of course, I am a little biased because I am her mom.

Francie had speech and cognitive delays at birth. She hated being touched. She did not cry or communicate with us. At the time we were in the military and had no diagnosis. I was trying hard to find ways to reach her but the doctors kept assuring me that there was nothing anyone could do and she would catch up. At age 4 a doctor finally told us she had Autism. Finally I had an enemy and a way to help her. I read everything and joined every group I could. Francie seemed to be responding to the things that the doctors said to do but she had little time to be a kid. She did not play like her older brother, instead she went to therapy- speech therapy, occupational therapy, and more. She was never at the park or at baseball practice.

The doctors suggested we try sign language and slowly Francie learned a few words. It took about three months and she started really trying to talk with us. Signing and talking suddenly made sense to Francie. She understood the basics of communication and we actually had conversations. Her speech was labored and she had a very small vocabulary but the day I heard her say, "Love Momma" was one of the best days of my life. After that Francie started to become the girl she was meant to be. She was discovering life in the way a newborn does, one slow step at a time.

Then one day while I was scrapbooking the world around us changed. Francie picked up the marker and stickers and started playing with it. I gave her more. She was scrapbooking right next to me. I told her teacher at school and they tried to get her to go to art class, and it worked. Suddenly Francie was interested in art and then communicating with the world. We encouraged the interest and her therapists worked with me using this new skill. Soon, therapy was a thing of the past.

Francie begged to go scrapbooking with me when I went to crops with my friends. I could not take her but she clearly wanted to go. She wanted to do art with friends like I did. So I started telling my friends who had children with and without disabilities. We started an informal playgroup where the kids could do art and explore their creative sides. People from all over the US donated their old art and scrapbooking supplies so the kids could continue their art projects. We talked to therapists who helped us plan projects so that the kids were getting what they needed without having to go to a boring office and play with adults. Here they could be kids and tell the world their stories.

Francie did just that. She wanted her story told. One day she decided to enter an art contest. I let her do it, knowing she did not have a chance to win. She did not win, but when she saw the art displayed at the mall in town, she asked where her art was. I tried to explain she did not win, but she was so sad. It got me thinking. Art was so important to her and she wanted the world to know. I was as proud of her art as the winning parents were but for different reasons. Her art took effort and told a story. If only someone could hear or see that story.

During this time I had become an advocate for parents with children with disabilities. I went back to school and got my masters in public policy administration. I volunteered with Parent to Parent of Georgia to help other parents so that no one would ever feel alone or frustrated with no answers like I had a few years ago. I wanted to make a difference. Francie had taught me so much and I wanted to show other parents that having a child with a disability was not a burden but a blessing. We found a way to do it. I called the museum in town and asked about the children's gallery where teachers often displayed their class's work. The museum gave me permission to have a small art display there. The volunteers from Parent to Parent in our city realized this idea had potential. The word spread and soon, we no longer were displaying only a few but 200 pieces of art! Children from all over our area, from schools, other non profits and the children's group we started got to display artwork for the whole month of October. The volunteers decided to make the artwork an awareness campaign. It needed a name and one of the leaders of the organization came up with "Beyond Expectations:

Artwork by Children with Disabilities" which was perfect, because the art show was beyond what we ever dreamed, but so was the art.

Francie's art teacher was inspired and started helping get all children into art classes at school, even the profoundly disabled kids who did not leave their classrooms. Their artwork was part of the show. The gala event for all the kids involved was one of the most memorable moments in my life and in many others. That night in October we saw children who never spoke lead their parents to their art, communicating for the first time. We saw kids socializing with other kids who had never made that effort before. We saw a young man's art career take off as he was featured in our show, one in New York, and got admitted into art school. We saw Francie proudly prance around the museum showing everyone her dreams realized- she had 3 pictures up on the wall of a museum – not the mall where any kids could win a contest, but in a museum next to real artists! She still holds the medal received that night with pride, and as she continues her art she is planning her new exhibit.

Beyond Expectations continues on this year. We are making preparations to make it a month long celebration of amazing kids. We know that the art show is more than awareness of disability in children. Francie taught us it is about pride, about belonging, about acceptance into her community.

This one amazing girl pushed me into being an advocate for other families like ours. She has helped me make a difference in our community and beyond.

The doctor who does family therapy recognized that not only did Francie have Autism but there were noticeable traits in her father and brother. So with my husband, son and daughter all being diagnosed with forms of Autism, I recognize the need in our community for more to be done.

I am working with Muscogee County Navigator Team a project of Parent to Parent on the second annual Beyond Expectations Art Show. We are hoping to help our community understand disability by awareness but also by acceptance of these amazing kids. Francie and the Art Show has influenced me in ways I never imagined. I had never met someone with a disability until I had a family. I never knew I could do so much and learn so much. I am now working on my doctorate in public policy. I volunteer full time to advocate for other families, and for all the children I know are out there. I am

 going beyond my own expectations in life. I am inspired to do more and be more. All because of a little girl who nobody knew could do anything. The first doctor told me to expect nothing from Francie. How wrong he was. She may need more time to learn, but I expect big things from her. I know now I will never limit anyone who has a disability. Instead I expect them to go beyond.

The Power of a Grandma

Polly Bouker

Recently company had been staying with us in our daughter's bedroom, so she had to move upstairs into the spare room. Unfortunately, this meant that she had to share a bathroom with our 10 year old son, Jonathan, who still races to the bathroom when he has to "go", and doesn't do such a great job of putting the seat up when he does "go." His sister was not thrilled about the surprise that she regularly found on the seat, but we just couldn't seem to get through to him about cleaning it before leaving the bathroom.

During that time, my parents were coming to visit for the day and I told Jon that he needed to help me clean the bathroom. Of course, as his eyes were glued to his favorite computer game, he seemed like he didn't hear me, until I said, "Grandma is going to have to use that bathroom!" At that, he jumped up from the computer and raced upstairs to help me clean.

I guess all we needed was Grandma!

Sticks and Stones Don't Mix with Cruise Ships

Teresa Johnson

"Sticks and stones may break my bones, but words will never hurt me". Remember those words we have said to ourselves as we have grown up and had mean and hurtful things said to or about us? We were taught, be tough, shake it off, don't let words hurt you. Well, they do hurt, and for many the pain is so deep, it is destructive.

We almost experienced the pain of losing our Rusty recently on a cruise back from the Bahamas. One of my greatest fears in taking this trip was that Rusty can be impulsive and unpredictable, especially if he was upset by something or someone. Being on a cruise ship in the middle of the Atlantic Ocean is no place for someone who is unpredictable. But, we went nonetheless with the hope that it was all just a bad "premonition" and I was over-reacting.

I wanted to hang on to him tightly, to not let him out of my sight, but there were other people from our church on this trip and there was a teen center on the ship so I let my guard down. We let him stay out later than usual, having to find him and make him come in on the first 2 nights, much to his disappointment. On Wed night, he stayed out to 2:30 am having the time of his life. I think he was having the most fun hanging out with some of the teens from church, the new youth pastor and playing cards, video games, etc. We had a false sense of security, but didn't realize it until Thursday night.

It was the final night of the cruise, and everyone wanted to make the most of that last night on the ship. Rusty asked to stay out with his friends and since the week had gone so well, we agreed. Around 12:30 p.m., our phone rang with an urgent call to come to the 12th deck, Rusty was upset. When John got to the top deck, Rusty was standing on the railing with intentions of jumping overboard. Details about what happened that led to this are sketchy, but some time earlier, some of the teen boys had made some remarks to Rusty that he would only say were "mean". Others also observed this, but didn't know enough about Rusty or how he would react to get involved. Rusty went to our music director who was on the trip with his family and asked to talk to him, but at some point, he climbed the rail with more than 1/2 of his body over the top, making a fall or jump very likely.

Over the course of a few moments, the music pastor was able to get close enough to him to pull him down and Rusty broke into sobs. Needless to say, we were up all night Thursday, concerned about him and also making sure he wouldn't decide to jump from our balcony in our room.

On Friday, we disembarked. Rusty has not said a word about who was involved or what was said. Only a comment from someone who overheard some of the things said by a couple of boys from church were relayed to us, so we don't have a full picture of what led to this occurrence. We do know one thing... Words can hurt, and cruise ships are not a place for someone who may react negatively to their environment.

Rusty was lucky, someone was there for him as many teens have lept to their death from cruise ships. I am thankful that God's hand was on him and we will be more cautious in every situation, regardless of pressure from others who think we are being too overprotective of him.

On the Team
JoEllen Hancock

All three of my children have special needs. Here is a story about one of my twin boys, Drew.

Drew recently turned 14 but is very small for his age. He has a skeletal growth delay of 24+ months. He underwent testing several years ago, which revealed that his body is unable to make sufficient growth hormones. So, he is roughly the size of a 4th or 5th grader. He only wears a size 10. In addition to his "vertical" challenges, he has OCD, ODD, Asperger's, Tourettes, Essential Tremor and Trichotillomania.

Needless to say, middle school was a challenge for him and toward the end of the year, an incident happened that was really bad for him. He is constantly bullied, picked on, made fun of, etc. You all know the story. You probably work with parents that tell you these same stories.

I was very concerned his freshman year of high school, because we were part of a redistricting into a new high school. It currently has only 9th grade as the actual building itself is not completely constructed. The building will open next year with 9th and 10th grades.

You can see my concern here, right? Transition from elementary into middle school. Rough. Transition into high school. Rough. Then transition again into the new building?

 A few weeks ago my son came to me and said he wanted to go out for the football team. While I want to encourage him to follow his dreams, the mom in me was scared he would become the target of all those kids who picked on him and because of his size, would become a target to hit on the field.

Well, he is now on the football team. The head coach is an amazing man who is a special education teacher and his philosophy is, "if you want to play for me, come on down!"

Because of his guidance, acceptance and attitude, I have actually seen a change in the attitudes of Drew's peers at school.

His first football game is soon and I will be sitting in the stands cheering!

Whether or not he ever gets any actual playing time on the field in a game doesn't really matter. Just the fact that he is being accepted and a member of the team is just fine with me! This coach has set the tone by teaching his team acceptance of all.

Ryan's Story
Beth Glotzbach

Ryan is one fun and amazing kid. Diagnosed with Autism at the age of 3, I knew in that moment our life's lessons were just starting and we were lucky to have been blessed with him to be in our lives.

We have been grateful, as he is very high functioning on the spectrum and tries hard to please his family and teachers. He always tries to do his best, which is all I ask of him. He requires patience and kindness to be able to achieve his fullest potential. He never wants to break the rules or disappoint. He wants to get good grades and knows it is hard and he must work twice as hard as others to accomplish this goal. He struggles socially. This is a part of autism that we have the most challenges with, and as he has gotten older it is the part where he realizes he is the most different.

If you ask him what autism is, he will tell you he has it, but does not really know what it is. Autism does not define who he is. What defines him is his creativity, his courage, and his likes and dislikes.

Ryan's world is his own, to be who he wants to be. He has a unique ability to transform himself into the characters of his favorite movies, performing scenes from Star Wars as if he really is a Jedi Knight. Some of his favorite things are small action figures, video games, his ipod, and his new cell phone. He never leaves the house without his books, especially on his weekly Friday visit to Kentucky Fried Chicken. He takes karate with such clarity and focus and will soon achieve the rank of Black Belt. We thank Mr. Thorton for giving of his time and patience. This is an amazing accomplishment. We are so proud of his hard work.

He believes that now being 13 entitles him to the rights of passage of being a teenager including picking on his younger sister Abby, growing facial hair, asking me often if he can shave yet, and even wanting a girlfriend. He is now taller than I am so trying to discipline him can be tough, as he is looking down at me. He told me the other day he is the Greatest Video Game player of all time, he loves cool movies and is the greatest Star Wars fan of all mankind. His words are enchanting as he described himself as fun, silly, confused at times, "but, I am a good person Mom!"

He will always tell you the truth, and his laugh is infectious. He has been taught mostly all things he knows, for learning does not come easy. The lessons he teaches us every day on how simple life should be are far greater. When he is trusting enough and comfortable he will let you into his world. He ends every night with, "Love you Mama" before bed and begins every morning with the question, "Mama I gotta ask you something" - moments I truly cherish.

Such work and ongoing success does not come without days of question, or concern about whether we have made the right choices. It has been 10 years since he was diagnosed. I often wonder where has the time gone.

Family and a few close friends are loving and supportive. Some people are not, which can take its toll on families. We try to help his sister Abby understand and make sure she knows she is important and we love her too. We stay within the limits that we know he can handle so that meltdowns are no longer an issue, if we just follow what works.

Most days are good and some days are more dreadful than others, and on those days it may take hours to get him back. On those days when I feel defeated, I try to remind myself how I came to be at peace with this. Perspective is a huge part of the world of autism. I am grateful he is here with us - he is my son, I must do all I can for him to grow into a good and honest man. I must encourage him to dream big and believe that he can do anything he sets his mind to. He just needs to be shown the way.

Autism is just a part of our children, it is not who they are.

McKenna
Annsley Genn

My name is Annsley Genn and I am 11 years old. My little sister's name is McKenna. When she was 3 years old, she was diagnosed with Rett Syndrome (which is a form of autism). She is now 7 years old and is an outgoing little girl. She enjoys laughing, dancing and running, but most of all, she loves taking showers!

We have a showerhead that you can take off and hold. McKenna also has a bath chair that she sits on in the shower. I get in with her and take the showerhead off and spray her and wash her hair. When I am done washing her, she will bend over in her chair and try to grab the water and put it in her mouth, and as we all know, that is nearly impossible. So she will sit there and try to grab the water for about 10 minutes, and then sit up to get sprayed. Then she bends back over to try to get the water. She has so much fun. I think that if my mom would let her, she would live in the shower!

Look at you now

Alisha McGlawn

About ten years ago, I would never know,

Just how much I'd watch you grow...

From tantrums and fights,

To sweet kisses goodnight----

I would never know---

Just how much you'd grow....

From a world of isolation, frustration and loneliness,

To participating in dance contests—

I never would have known---

Just how much you would have grown!

From screams, noises and incomprehensible speech,

To new words and utterances every single week---

Oh my, how much you've grown!

I never would have known!

From blank stares, which seemed to gaze right past me.

To loving glances that embrace, and encourage me!

My God, look at how much you have grown---

I think that I have always known--

The beauty that was hidden inside—

Just waiting to be revived---

Newly awakened strengths, talents and abilities—

Coming out of you—for the whole world to see!

Look at you now!!!

A dedication to Christian---Who continues to grow!

Victor's Decathlon Speech
Victor Alvarado

Some kids that have brothers or sisters with autism hate them because they can't do anything at home with their friends or go anywhere because of them. It makes me sad to know that, because there are a lot of people who love their sons, daughters, brothers, or sisters with autism.

I know when people find out that their child has autism it really makes them heartbroken, because they know that their child is most likely to not live a normal life. But my family is one of families that believe that we can recover Julian from autism. Julian and the many other children that are burdened and blessed with this terrible of all diseases are all very special. My brother Julian is one of the many miracles that have happened to our family. Only through guidance, love, acceptance, and determination will we be able to find a way to defeat autism.

Dad finds it hard to go out with us because he doesn't like when Julian makes noises and when people stare at us when we are at the store, a restaurant, or any other public place. Well, would you like it when people give mean comments or weird looks at your family member?

My sister in-law is afraid Julian will hurt my nephew, Noah accidentally. He likes to play with us but he doesn't realize that he's playing rough. She loves Julian but she really never takes the time to get to know him and understand him more.

Just because he doesn't talk doesn't just mean he has nothing to say. It's really hard for us when people can only see the negative side of autism and not the beauty of the person.

A question my mom always talks about is who will take of Julian if he still needs care once she passes away. Sometimes I see or feel that Julian seems to get more of my parent's affection, which makes me wonder, "Does having a brother with autism mean my parents love him more than the rest of us?" My mom told me she realizes that we feel neglected because of my brother, but it's just that he needs that little extra attention so he knows that we care for him too.

My dad and I have teamed up to together to teach Julian how to take of himself, now the he is a young man. My mom's baby has grown up and she feels that he needs his privacy and dignity. But most of the time, I am usually the one teaching him the basic things that we need to know. Over the past years I have shown him how to bathe himself, clothe himself, brush his teeth, and how to eat with a spoon or a fork instead of his hands. I also taught him how to work our VCR and DVD player.

The experiences I have had with Julian are difficult and pleasant all the same and are very rewarding, especially when he hugs me, kisses on the cheek and wants to play with me. For all the boys and girls who have siblings with autism, I hope reading this will encourage them not to be embarrassed of their siblings with autism, but help them to be more supportive and to help their siblings be successful.

Whenever I hear how other families are hurting and struggling, I feel a little bit sympathetic because each family has their own experiences, which can be positive, negative, or both. In our family we have both, but more with positive than negative.

Ty

Lysa Marchand

Ty was diagnosed with autism at the age of 2 years and 5 months. The signs came much earlier.

He was an infant when I knew that something about him was different than his twin sister. It's funny how a mother knows, even though it might break your heart to hear it out loud. I remember feeling a sense of relief when the 3 specialists sat in front of my husband and me and said that Ty was autistic, and then incredible sadness about 15 minutes later.

I think it was more for the fear of how I was going to be able to help him. I could barely understand what it was like to be autistic. He couldn't tell me; he was barely talking at that point (and at 5 and a half he still can't tell me). I had the feeling that we had to act right away, starting the healing process with interventions, such as speech and occupational therapies. I remember having so many meltdowns in those early days feeling I was going to fail him. I so didn't want to fail him.

As time went on I realized I had to make my goals smaller, and not so overwhelming. One was to get him to kiss me again. He stopped giving kisses shortly after I went back to work (around 1 year after they were born). It broke my heart. I made it my mission, smothering him with kisses from the moment I got in the door (seriously, the kid smelled like spit). It took months, but one day he leaned in and touched his head to mine and that was enough. I knew what he meant. I gradually evolved to lips touching my cheek, to kissing me and him saying "t-ma" out loud (to simulate the sound of a kiss).

Then about a month ago we were cuddling and I asked him to give me a "smacker". I kissed him and made the kissy sound on his cheek. He responded with the loudest smacker kiss you have ever heard! He's my love bug, I have always told him he makes me "cozy in my heart" so he would understand what my love for him feels like and he now responds by saying "mommy,you make me cozy in my heart too".

Never give up on your child...whether they can talk or not, they can feel your love and sometimes if you are persistent enough, they will show it back. It may not be how other kids do but you will find that it will be in there own special way and it is more than enough.

It really is a Wonderful World
Polly Bouker

When Jon was 6, we wanted to take a family trip to Disney World. I had read about other families with autistic children going there and having a great time. We really wanted to do this "normal" family activity and to give Hannah and Jon the experience of Disney while they were small enough to really appreciate the "magic." As always, we were worried about whether or not Jon could do it, and whether or not we would be able to manage him.

That July, we stayed for a few days at the Disney Fort Wilderness Campground. On the evening that we first arrived, we took the ferry over to the Magic Kingdom to show the kids where we would be going the next two days. They were so excited that they even had a great time just riding the Monorail through the Disney Properties!

The next morning, we headed to the Magic Kingdom, with Guest Services as our first planned stop. I had read that if you bring a letter from your child's doctor that children with autism could get a

special access pass to many of the rides at Disney. I had my letter ready as I approached the counter with Jon bouncing off the walls all around me. As often happens when he is very excited, he was repeating things over and over, and was making his typical loud shrieks and other noises. Before I could even get the letter onto the counter, the Disney representative was asking me how many were in my family, and how long we planned to be at their park. He handed over the pass, and very kindly said, "I'm glad I could help." If he only knew.

At that point we really didn't know that the Guest Assistance Pass would do for us. What we quickly found was that a quick wave of the pass got our family into Disney's FastPass lines at various rides. At the Pirates of the Caribbean ride, we were quickly swept away through a gate into the behind the scenes area where we quite literally "ran into" Dr. Hook and one of the Chipmunks. Jon and Hannah were delighted! We continued on through a back door into the attraction, where we quickly reached the area to board the boats and felt very special. At the Haunted Mansion, we were whisked away into a secret passageway that bypassed the lines as we were taken to the start of the ride. Again, we were treated as if we were VIPs!

Those two days were magical. While we had to deal with incredible heat, crowds, Jon's meltdowns in the middle of the Magic Kingdom, and the damage to our wallets, this was a family vacation that was even better than it would have been if we didn't have a child with autism.   Jon's "golden boy" status there proved to be an unexpected benefit of being the parent or sibling of someone with autism.   Even his sister appreciated his autism for those couple of days!

BLESSED
Diana Olivarria Alvarado

My son is disabled I am blessed.
That makes no sense, is what you say.

My son is speechless, I am blessed.
In this case silence is not golden, is what you say.

My son cannot call me mama, I am blessed.
You shake your head in sadness, you have nothing to say.

My son always plays alone, I am blessed.
Where is the pleasure in that, is what you say.

My son has some quirky behaviors, I am blessed.
You need to be stern, is what you say.

My son was created by a living GOD, I am blessed.
How can you still have faith, is what you say.

Seven days a week my faith lives in my son,

I am BLESSED.

My son was injured by the vaccines,
Now he is blessed.

My son kisses and hugs us,
We are blessed.

My son is a magnet for strangers prayers,
They are blessed.

My son can conquer mountains,
He is blessed.

My sons eyes are the doorway to his soul,
He is blessed.

My son knows JESUS in the purest form,
He is blessed.

If my son has touched you heart,
You have been

BLESSED.

Warrior
Sue Hansen

The Warrior in Room G340, Emory University Hospital....

Sean currently has wires all over his head, and they are not topical. These wires are embedded in his brain, put there surgically with a grid at his request to Dr. Robert Gross of Emory University Hospital. The wires remind me of "The Matrix" movie, when people are in vats of liquid and they are wired from their heads to a machine that feeds them the illusion of a full and complete life.

Seeing Sean sitting in the bed next to me reminds me that it was not that long ago that my husband Mike and I were given him as a gift, our very own Sean Michael, on November 5, 1986. He was a blonde haired, blue-eyed beauty. Our gift came later with some surprises. Sean read at the wee age of two, put puzzles together faster than adults as a toddler, in third grade had photographic recall of anything he read, and we learned he read with both eyes reading both sides of the book simultaneously. I don't remember ever reading War and Peace in 3rd grade, but my son did. In fact, he is very well read as you might guess.

Unfortunately some of the surprises our gift had were not as welcomed. His seizures began when he was 4 years old. Sean began to lose his place in conversation during one week and by the end of the next week he was having 20 seizures a day. In third grade this brilliant mixture of gifts and struggles was also diagnosed as autism.

In the press lately are the books about Warrior Mothers and autism. I see it differently, although I did everything I could for my son, even founding a camp for autism when he was nine. I always felt that he was the warrior. I was the mother of a true hero, a warrior. He was like no other child - smart, gifted, and unique and willing to overcome his obstacles. Even at the age of five he wanted pants with pockets so he would quit flapping his hands and put them in his pocket (so the other kids would quit mocking him). So when Sean decided he wanted to live his life to the fullest and not be fed illusions, I agreed with him.

So, our planned Hansen family summer of 2009 included a month in the hospital, a well planned summer around brain surgeries and the hope of Sean's freedom. Sean's brother Zach, our other gift was willing to give his summer up to give his brother his freedom. Zach has his own stories and he came when we needed him most! Sean wanted to have the surgery to eradicate the seizures, although I was scared, we all wanted this for him too.

I remember being eighteen and having my own car, a '72 Camaro. With driving came freedom to get an education of my choice. I had the option to get a job wherever I wanted to go. Freedom is something my warrior has not experienced. Unfortunately because he has no freedom he also lacks the quality of life he deserves. Why should my warrior not have the same opportunities I had? So my husband and I backed Sean on his decision to do this risky but hopeful surgery. Of course my acceptance of the surgery comes with a request for many prayers. Lucky for me, I work at Marist Catholic School in Atlanta. We pray a lot there.

Sean was clearly saying he wanted the gift of freedom and he did not want to be linked to anticonvulsants and seizure-causing barriers for the rest of his life. He wants to get his driver's license and get a 1980's BMW, and eventually drive across the country seeing friends and relatives, free as a bird. We want that for him as well.

For 18 years Sean has had seizures daily, obviously not to be outgrown as we once hoped. We started the screening process with Dr. Helmers and Emory in August 2008 when we moved Sean to live with us in Atlanta. He could see the specialists at Emory University Hospital and recuperate in our home. After 4 different MRI's and some psychological tests, Sean was allowed to proceed further as a good candidate for the surgery. The process for this surgery was long and we were all getting tired of the long waits in between tests, but when you are known for being the best, there is usually a line. In the process of this wait and tests Sean has agreed to be parts of two studies to further the science of brain study. He wants to help the next guy in his quest for freedom!

In May, we finally met with Dr. Robert Gross, Emory brain surgeon extraordinaire. What I like about Dr. Gross besides his credentials and experience is his ability to light up a room when he smiles. Dr.

Gross understood the wait that Sean has gone through for this procedure and gave us an early July date. On the 22nd we had the first surgery, a grid installed on his brain with wires coming out that went to a monitoring board. We waited for seizures and when they came we found out that the right temporal was not the seizure location.

Sean went in for another procedure on the 29th to have another grid placed in the frontal lobe and down the middle of his brain. This grid had even more wires to monitor and the results were that the source of the seizures might be coming from the left frontal lobe. We are not sure what the next steps are but in our urging to have him allow seizures to come we become surer of their origination. We will wait for the Consultation Team to decide the route of surgery and the best method. Of course all the while I will be praying.

 I am writing this story while Sean sits by my side in room 340 G of the Epilepsy Monitoring Unit of Emory Hospital in Atlanta. We are here 24 hours a day at the hospital, with my husband and I alternating our shifts for two weeks now. A machine that looked a lot like a Mackie Sound Board with the data going to a central computer in the hallway is tucked in a bag, on a computer stand with wheels - A partner to Sean right now. He also has a video recorder aimed at his bed and a 50-foot cord that allows him a small radius to travel within the room.

The most ironic part of this process is our unusual encouragement for Sean to have as many seizures as he can possibly summon. For example, I did not know that You Tube had a seizure video you could download to induce seizures, but apparently there are many.

When Sean is at home he has them quite often, especially when he is in his creative mode. Writing for hours and hours at a time with no sleep in sight, Sean could have 4 on any given day.

As we wait we hope for the best and we continue to pray for a good surgery and a freedom that is what the doctor ordered. My hope is that Sean, unlike those in the Matrix, is not fed illusions, but is instead given a chance at a life my warrior deserves.

Finding Kyle

Greg Perry

I am searching for Kyle;
I find him more each day;
I am finding Kyle in his:
    Huge Smile
        Hug and pat
    Laugh and giggle
        Sparkling Eyes
    Footsteps
        Gentle kiss and nuzzling
    Puzzled expression
        Waving goodbye
    Splashing in the tub
        Getting bath water on the floor
    Swinging around and around on the rope swing
        Clogging the toilets weekly
    Squeezing out all the toothpaste in the house
        Turning down the music because, "No like"
    Turning up the music because, "Like"
        Watching Blues Clues for 100th time
    Climbing up on top of the grandfather clock

Winding the grandfather clock daily
Breaking the grandfather clock wires and pendulum
Hiding the key to the grandfather clock
Taking the weights off the grandfather clock
Flushing keys and Hot Wheels down the toilet
Unrolling all the toilet paper in the house
Playing in the bathroom sinks
Playing with the water hose and dragging it on the flowers
Leaving the faucet on for four days
Changing clothes after getting a little bit dirty
Shooting basketball for hours
Chasing Lizzy with his 'Peanut' riding toy
Breaking door knobs by sticking items in the hole
Setting off the car alarms with the remote at all hours
Reading him a story
Sleeping with him with his leg across my chest
Sneaking into our bed with dirty feet
Demanding his hot dog be cut precisely correct
Drinking out of the dog's bowl
Putting his food in the dog's bowl and eating it
Feeding Lizzy Dog his food and saying, "Gone"
Eating big bags of candy while hiding from us
Never calling me "Daddy", only "Greg"
Playing with the ice maker – ice all over the floor
Turning the ceiling fan on and off
Turning lights on and off repeatedly
Opening and swinging on the refrigerator door
Letting the dog out and urgently telling us to catch her
Putting inappropriate items in the dryer
Putting a cell phone in the washer
Turning on the stove and watching the eye turn
red
Telling us, "Be careful of the cars"
Giving us goodbye kisses on each cheek

Eating burritos and PJ sandwiches daily
       Putting metal in the microwave
Starting a fire in the microwave by cooking his own burrito
       Always wanting chicken nuggets and 'fren' fries
Eating, running, jumping, throwing up and starting over
       Puking at Frankie G's restaurant every time he
       goes
Touching and feeling the stereo speakers' vibrations
       Collecting compact discs and building towers
Selecting and listening to music on the radio and stereo
       'Turtling' his car seat with himself in it – flipping it
Opening and closing the electric car door with his toes
       Being bossy and bouncy
Having mom still spoon feed him yogurt
       Saying, "Play with me; Now!"
Saying, "Slow Poke, Slow Poke, Na Na Na Na Slow Poke"
       Reading 'Swan Sky' & repeating the "Qua, Qua"
Lining up crayons in intricate patterns and designs
       Filling up water cups and pouring them out
Watching the planes land and take-off at the airport
       Smiling upon waking
Putting salt and pepper in the toaster
       Eating all the popsicles and cheese slices
Assuring you, "This is my last one" – "pop-pullcul"
       Bring a diaper and lying down for you
Getting in the car just to back up in the driveway
       Tying the blinds around the curtain rod
Tearing down the blinds and destroying them
       Eating your snow cone instead of his
Throwing his toys out the window
       Always picking out Life Saver Gummies
Opening candy packages by himself and spilling them
       Getting angry if you interrupt his routine
Having to always open the gate, "Me first"
       Saying, "I went to Lit' Red School House today"

Saying, "Have a good weekend" every time he leaves
　　　　Locking you in the laundry room
Locking his door after 9:00 pm to play
　　　　Saying, "Get out of my room; I want to play"
Constantly listening to Calypso music
　　　　Jumping on the trampoline
Knowing when he is about to "puke up"
　　　　Running to his room, locking the door to avoid
　　　　you
Saying, "I be good; I be good now; I be good tomorrow"
　　　　Asking, "Where's mom, dad, Ali, Katie, Chad…."
Always wanting to say the blessing at dinner
　　　　Praying to bless everyone he knows and his toys
Wanting to keep your phone in his pocket
　　　　Getting Katie's ipod and knowing how to work it
Wanting his Disney 'Nemo' cover, not sleeping without it
　　　　'Gusher' grabbing and hiding for later
Spraying cologne until emptying the bottle
　　　　Wanting outside to ring the door bell
Sliding around in the tub after the water drains
　　　　Climbing on and up the metal bed
Throwing the ball up and down repeatedly for hours
　　　　Saying, "Its okay; I'm ok" when he falls
Untying his shoes
　　　　Destroying his shoelaces
Telling everyone, "Dr. Aljabi fixed my arm"
　　　　Repeatedly identifying his previous injuries
Strumming a guitar again and again; he does not play
　　　　Pulling down dad's ties
Unrolling the deodorant until it falls out
　　　　Pulling out all the dental floss
Bouncing the big balls at the chiropractor
　　　　Not wearing pants
Prancing about in his underwear or nude, even outside
　　　　Telling others to "Say excuse you when you fart"

Not wanting his hair washed
> Stopping to throw sticks and rocks in the pond

Stopping our walks to swing in the neighbor's swing
> Lying down on the dock to put his hand in the water

Stooping down to talk into the storm drains
> Circling, circling and circling on his bicycle

Always racing and answering the phone with, "Who is it?"
> Liking pressure on his body - the "Mash me" game

Typing over mom's doctorial thesis on the computer
> Turning the printer on and off jamming the paper

Staring into water fountain exhaust vents
> Staring, watching the fans in air conditioner units

Putting balloons in the ceiling fans
> Hitting the ceiling fans with brooms and balls

Plugging and unplugging guitar cables while you play
> Taking mom's clothes off the hangers

Arranging clothes hangers on the end table
> Standing and dancing on the piano keys

Feeding Cheeko by dumping out good food daily
> Opening Cheeko's birdcage and leaving

Playing with any object with sound
> Using up 50 to 60 AA batteries per month

Approving of his lunch and telling you with a nod
> Handing me things I do not need

Copying you in a constant game of 'Simon – NOT- Says'
> Wanting his back rubbed

Playing chiropractor on your toes when wanting his pulled
> Hanging out with the big boys

Playing with flashlights and leaving them on
> Pulling the hanging light out of the ceiling

Climbing into the attic to turn the light off on you
> Making Blaze (rocking horse) hop across the room

Saying, "A little bit longer snuggle in bed"

Ringing the door bell until the battery dies

Turning the stereo down because "It's too 'noise'"

Getting up and turning off the lights when tired

Completing a task and clapping, saying, "I did it, I did"

Dancing with the birds on Blue's Clues video

Playing games according to his own rules

Singing Beatles' songs and kids' songs

Having a Rod Stewart hair style every morning

Pulling weather stripping off the front door

Quivering lower lip when he gets scolded

Wearing a dirt necklace – a dirt line on his neck

Playing coy and looking back over his shoulder smiling

Trimming the Christmas tree with scissors

Blowing soap bubbles and wanting you to catch them

Saying, "Your turn Greg" then going again himself

Getting knocked down by ocean waves and laughing

Locking himself accidentally in the shed

Ignoring and turning his back saying, " I 'heared' nothing"

Putting his unwanted dinner in the toilet

Playing with all automatic doors

Pushing the grocery cart into people and displays

Hugging the day school staff before leaving for home

Collecting all rocks he can find

Saying, 'You don't boss me around'

Opening the front door to let flying bugs inside

Climbing over and under pews at church

Making funny faces and 'twisty' movements

Looking into your eyes and 'big eyeing' you

Saying, "I love you; you're my best friend"

Burning toast in the 'forbidden – don't touch it' toaster

Spraying bleach and paint into the dryer, on
clothes

Riding his bike to the edge of the driveway teasingly

Turning the lights on in the van and leaving

Changing the video to Barney in the middle of your movie

89

Sleeping with you with his nasty feet in your face
Wanting the ipod to only play 'Help' by the Beatles
Angrily spraying me with the water hose
Thanking God "that I don't put things in the dryer now"
Greeting people with "Your butt stinks"
Throwing up in the car after drinking orange soda
Singing 'I Want to Hold Your Hand' in English
Constantly wanting a hair cut and doing it himself
Sneaking two extra books in to be read
Rubbing music discs he does not like on the brick porch
Showing he loves you by rubbing your upper arm
Insisting on playing 'Hide-n-Seek' in the house
Eating Peanut Butter and Jelly on Raisin Bread
Hanging upside down on the swing and spinning off it
Wanting to go to 'Old McDonald's' for a meal
Chewing on the steering wheel and damaging it
Telling the teacher, "LEAVE the music on"
Watching the movie 'Beauty Shop' over and over again
Only wearing his 'light-up' shoes
Wanting to go to the pool with mom
Listening to his yodel – "AAAAAH, AAAAAH"
Hiding from mom when she returns after leaving him home
Dancing on the piano keys
Singing Beatles' songs, knowing the words - unlike mom
Blaming us for lightning knocking out the lights
Kicking a student in class after she got the kick ball
Seeking attention by acting ugly and disruptive
Wrapping a belt around the ceiling fan to watch it wind up
Getting very bored in class
Loving to ride the bus and smiling when the bus arrives
Locking himself in the bathroom stall at school
Refusing to open that door making the teacher crawl under
Hitting redial and calling people repeatedly
Loving mom's animal sounds while feeding him yogurt

Knock knees

Leaving the lunch table to watch the tray conveyer belt

Fascination with sprinklers

Asking, "Where we go" if we just want him to wear clothes

Putting his underwear on backwards

Being a 'bobble head' stuttering for a 'last piece' of candy

Swinging on the rope every day waiting for the
bus

Building a wall out of the dvd's and video tapes

Wetting the trampoline before jumping on it

Getting a can opener and randomly opening many cans

Cooking mom's cell phone in the microwave

Tying his Spiderman to the ceiling fan and turning it on

Watering flowers until they drown

Wandering off on Halloween night with other 'creatures'

Filling up the frig with re-filled bottles of water

Running the sink until it overflows to create a water fall

Washing clothes and putting in too much
detergent

Flooding the laundry room with water and soap suds

Mixing all snack foods into one large plastic bag

Walking by the TV and turning your movie off

Saying, "I watch Me–ka mao-se" – Mickey Mouse

Laughing, and saying 'dair are no messages',

Listening to phone messages over and over for
days

Getting angry if you erase any phone messages

Wanting macaroni and cheese at every meal

Playing with 'Hot Wheels Crisscross Crash' game

Spilling sugar all over the floor

Throwing his lunch box down when the food is not exact

Watching the same 15 seconds of video 20 times

Telling you to "sit down crisscross applesauce"

Shooting the Hoppy ball in the basketball goal

Spinning in the hanging chair until it falls out of the ceiling

Throwing balls into the fan and bouncing them off
Wanting to stop at every playground he sees
Screaming at the top of his lungs when mad
Hitting Stephanie when she returns after leaving him home
Running, smiling and locking you outside
Always asking 'Where's Mom?' even when she is home
Leaving battery powered toys on to kill the batteries
Washing the same dishes and clothes over and over
Being obsessed with Thomas and Percy toy trains
Telling you the expressions of Thomas the Tank Engine
Not using the track for his trains – free range toys
Spraying bathrooms with removable shower heads
Spraying mom down when in her Sunday best
Saying, "Where you going?" when you put on a shirt
Painting the wall in the hall with magic markers
Turning on a public PA system and singing his tunes
Doing his autistic stomp to flushing toilets
Climbing up the arbor to play with the wind chimes
Wanting a hair cut every time he sees the clippers
Climbing and hanging on the basketball goal naked
Eating out of the dog's pan
Knowing what music he likes in seconds of playing a disc
Throwing discs out when he does not like the music
Playing with new puzzles for hours and days
Telling you to be quiet during 'his' video / dvd
Wanting you to watch the same video with him repeatedly
Wallowing on and jumping on you in the bed
Kicking you and the bed covers off at night
Praying with his head down in the dinner chair
Jumping off the metal bed headboard at the ceiling fan
Only drinking orange Hi C punch, nothing else
Rearranging the doctor's office and riding the swivel stool
Jumping on kids' heads in the pool

92

Moving the doctor's chair and table while it was being used

Sitting on top of the refrigerator

Opening and closing the foot operated trash can into a wall

Drinking out of the cartons and leaving 'floaters'

Driving a remote control car to the edge of the stairs

Saying, 'It gonna fall, it gonna fall down'

Speeding and sliding the peanut to the edge of the stairs

Playing the 'You Imitate Me' game

Pushing toys off the stairs to get them to land upside down

Liking school lunches

Poking along very intentionally while the bus waits for him

Wearing his great BIG backpack to the bus

Hiding his bag if he acted bad at school – bad behavior note

Eating ice cream from the container, leaving it out

Demanding the windshield wipers be on at all times

Wearing a cherry snow cone mustache

Leaving his room and coming to you after being disciplined

Tormenting you on purpose, knows your buttons

Putting sticks and leaves in the AC unit and overheating it

Slapping windows when you leave & cracking them

Cutting his own toe nails back to the flesh causing pain

Not being so wild for other people, just us

Bouncing basketballs off the hood of the car

Climbing up on the van luggage rack

Getting under the couch cushions, wanting to be mashed

Cramming crackers into the cd player

Standing in the kitchen naked eating a cupcake

Urinating in the middle on the living room floor

Saying, "See you in 5 minutes" when leaving for the day

Having smelly breath in the morning and proving it

Sharing the ipod earpiece with you as he listens too

Wearing Dutch wooden shoes on the wooden floor

Sharing candy with you and putting pieces in your mouth

Chasing and trying to step on a balloon

Playing 'in a cave and tunnel' under the sheets with you

Pulling down all the crepe paper from his party

Taping pieces of crepe paper to the ceiling fan to swirl

Getting excited about his cake

Insisting that you re-light the birthday candles many times

At times saying, 'Turn off the tv, it's time for bed'

Always saying, "I want 'chick nugs' at OLD McDonald's"

Getting vise grips hung on his finger

Playing the magnetic attraction game, dividing the pieces

Calling a fireplace fire 'the little fire'

Shaking his head, rolling his eyes & wah-wah'ing – a game

Urinating on the floor for vengeance and retribution

Not complaining when cleaned off with a cold wet wipe

Saying, "Greg, I love Jishuku" – the magnet game

Insisting you whisper the 'BOO' in the Hippo Hiccup book

Saying when batteries are low, "They are sick"

Taking off and replacing ornaments on the Christmas tree

Declaring, "Thomas the Tank engine is slow sick"

Breaking door knobs by cramming items in the holes

Remaining asleep in the morning while I dress him

Hanging his handmade ornaments only on the tree's front

Insisting his ornaments be at his eye level

Calling 'Joe the Bear & Sam the Mouse' his BooWho book

Working the fog machine and light show at church

Saying, "Santa is coming to see me, I am a good boy"

Turning all the snow globes on at once

Crying when told, "Santa doesn't come to visit bad boys"

His making 'Puppy Eyed Please' face

Singing Santa Claus is coming to town, acting the parts

Running to show Santa his picture with Kyle

Saying he "had a good first day at school" each afternoon
Flushing every toilet he meets
Pretending he is a piano that you play to cell phone rings
Loving the color orange, using only that crayon
Pushing the teachers and other students in his class
Pushing chairs over in class when angry
Climbing under the table and hiding during speech class
Carrying a picture of he and his mom in his pack
Painting the tops of the solar walkway lights teal
Lying on and riding the skateboard in the house
Stopping and staring at every vending machine he passes
Riding his bike around the inside of the house
Loving to go on bike rides and nature walks
Cutting his own hair one day before school
pictures
Cutting his hair saying, "My hair is not strong anymore"
Walking around the house with a slice of bologna
Asking, "Can I watch you?" when you are concentrating
Telling me "not to pick him up' from after school
Saying over and again, "I like my haircut; it's pretty"
Breaking three door handles to the new van
Saying, "cry" as he rolls over our hand prints in the cement
Fixing a drink, taking one sip, pouring it out
Bring a fan, pointing it at me because 'I need air'
Only wearing orange colored tennis shoes
Picking clothes for school upon getting home from school
Saying "ask" verses "tell" what happened
Singing part of "I Want to Hold Your Hand" in German
Crying and hating having to learn the alphabet
Putting marbles in a flip drawer, opening it, spilling them
Saying each day, "Ali not take her truck to college"
Grabbing my hand on hearing "I Want to Hold Your Hand"
Repeatedly washing the hardwood floor with
water
Wetting the table, watching it dry to pick out shapes

Saying, "It very" "stinks / taste good / . . . . ."
Saying, "There is stink coming out of your mouth"
Yelling in church, "Who farted?" when no one has
Cramming his pack full of toys and carrying it to school
Mixing Kool Aid on the floor 'without a pitcher'
Seeing 3 kids swimming, saying, "There should be 4" - him
Being able to swallow his medicine and being
proud
Playing 'I'm <u>not</u> your best friend' with his older brother
Insisting daily, "I go Summer Waves" Water Park"
Double dipping a chip until it falls apart in the salsa
Loving to go through car washes
Always wanting his picture taken and then looking at it

And in
discovering him in his
Just being Kyle, just being Totally Kyle –
a Kyle of God

Kyle is a gift from God. Kyle brings us daily gifts from Heaven.

We
enjoy him, love him, play with him and bathe him frequently.
We would not have him any other way.

96

A trip to the Dentist

Teresa Johnson

The dentist was never one of my favorite places to visit as a child. It's just one of those "necessary evils" we have to go through in life and you do it because you know you have to, not because you want to.

Rusty was never the best patient at the dentist either. He fought a highly recommended children's dentist and wouldn't let his teeth be checked or cleaned. Of course, as a 3 year old who had undiagnosed autism at the time, we just assumed he needed to be put into a papoose and he would be fine. Not so. We tried anti-anxiety medication to relax him;, it wired him even more. Then we learned Rusty had autism at age 4. I tried to be more understanding, but the dentist disregarded the psychological report and continued to restrain Rusty in spite of his emotional meltdowns. My oldest son would try to console his brother; it upset him greatly. (Parents had to stay in the waiting room in this office) After a very exhausting experience one day where Rusty was screaming inconsolably and soaked with sweat, I exchanged a few words with the dentist (something about "traumatizing my child") and he suggested we find another dentist. My thoughts exactly!

That was easier said than done. Just how many dentists were there in Atlanta? And how many were willing to work with children on the autism spectrum? Very few! We went to Children's Healthcare of Atlanta and found a dentist who worked with physically and developmentally disabled children. During one of the visits, this dentist recommended that Rusty would need a retainer as one of his front teeth was coming in wrong. It was sticking almost straight out. Rusty was a thumb sucker and at this time, he was in the 3rd grade. Getting a mold for the retainer was quite the experience. He thought he was going to die; still the dentist was very calm with him through the whole process.

On the day he received his retainer his anxiety level was through the roof. The dentist put it in, giving me strict instructions "DO NOT TAKE THIS OUT". I listened to Rusty screaming, having an extreme meltdown, and I was carrying him to the car with everyone within hearing distance staring at me as if I had kidnapped him. I talked softly to him and he would scream. I ignored him, and he would scream louder. I thought I was going to have a wreck on the way home because of the fit he was throwing saying "Take it out, take it out NOW!" I told him how cute he was going to be when his tooth was fixed and he screamed, "I like my tooth". It was nerve wracking, but I had to keep my sense of humor on the drive home.

What I failed to mention was this was 5 o'clock on a Friday afternoon in the pouring rain on I-285 in Atlanta traffic. It was also my birthday. The funniest part about this whole story is that Rusty was so upset he kept telling me "I hope you have an UNHAPPY Birthday". Even though I was stressed to the max, just thinking about him telling me that all the way home (for over almost 2 hours in traffic) I had to laugh about it.

The outcome: He did wear it for about a year and his teeth are beautiful (he's almost 18). Dentist visits were and continue to be an upsetting ordeal; he is now put to sleep for any dental work. Oh, I did have many more happy birthdays!

Figure it out as you go
Polly Bouker

Jon is a "runner."

Like so many children with autism, he can be walking along just fine and then suddenly bolts. He is also strong - I mean *strong* like those stories you hear about people having super human strength in an emergency.   Only, Jon's super human strength occurs when he wants to do something or wants to have something and I don't agree.

Let's just say, I am not an Olympic sprinter or weightlifter. I was 31 when Jon was born, so as he got bigger and faster, I was certainly beyond my best sprinting age. Although I consider myself strong for a small person, it won't be long before he has more strength than me.   I've had to come up with some super human strength, too.

Over the years, many well meaning people have asked me questions such as "What will you do when he is a teenager?" or

"Why not just let him run around and get tired?" or "Will you be able to continue to take him places?" I don't know what I will do when he is a teenager. He doesn't get tired, and only gets more revved up if I let him run around. I certainly hope that I can continue to take him out to experience life. Being trapped at home is easier in many ways, but isn't really a very good answer. He is disabled, but he is no less of a person than anyone else and needs to experience life. The world has to meet me halfway, don't they?

Like parents of many kids with disabilities, my husband and I certainly don't have all the answers. But, then again we haven't had the answers for what to do in situations with our daughter (who is not disabled) *until we were living them*. The same goes for life with a child with autism. *We figure it out as we go.*

When Jon could no longer fit in a stroller, we were pretty worried. My parents live in Mexico, so a simple visit to see Grandma and Grandpa involves long immigration and customs lines on both ends of the trip. Going through post 9/11 airport security and dealing with crowds and noise, and getting to other parts of the airport for connecting flights with little time to spare are just some of what we had to face. Could we do this with Jon, considering his unexpected running and strength?

One day, we realized that we could try putting Jon in a wheelchair for traveling. He wouldn't have to know that we were thinking of it as a big stroller. It turned out that he loved it. As a matter of fact, he and Hannah both wanted to ride in it. Jon sits in it and holds some of our bags on his lap as we race across the terminal. Several years later, we are still using the wheelchair and have expanded to using it in other places when we worry about him getting away.

We don't know if he will accept the wheelchair forever, but for now, we've figured out a way to give him more of life's experiences.

The Moriarty challenge
Timothy and Dawn Moriarty

Our story is about the challenges and the struggles that parents face with having a child with autism. Our family consists of all three of our children on the severe side of the spectrum. Starting at the beginning is the diagnosis of our first child; it was quite devastating. The loss and grief was relentless. Looking back - calling to find out some answer or to find out what exactly is involved with having a child with autism, looking for some clue or maybe some cure to this diagnosis. I will never forget the words from a volunteer worker who told me to "get ready for the biggest fight of your life."

Only then, I did not know what our life had in store for us. About a year later, after trying to pick up the pieces and alter our life with our daughter, our twin boys also started to show signs similar to those of our daughter when they were about 15 months old. Soon enough we had a diagnosis for our twin boys as well. We never expected twins and did not know how to handle twin boys with autism? Where? What? How?

Depression, anxiety and hopelessness were always with us from morning till night until we learned more and more about autism. We needed to fight for our children so they could have a life just like any other child. We learned to deal with our situation after hiding our feelings for a very long time. We have been through a great ordeal but we are very proud of our children with every day that goes by.

It seems to me that children with autism are very hard workers, just to get from each small step to another. To us as parents it feels like every time a goal is reached, or even a small gesture of a smile or a hug is priceless.

We have no respite and have been on waiting lists for many years and many people say, "Oh help is on its way." It has been years but we always find the strength to carry on, as does as any other family.

It might be a different life or an unusual life but it's ours and we are very proud of all the efforts we take to make this family what it is today. Our daughter is now 11 yrs old and even after all the challenges she has overcome, is still nonverbal and not fully potty trained. She has learned to communicate using the pec system. She is a loving girl and has many likes and dislikes just as anyone else. She loves to go to school and is the first towards the door. Our twin boys have just turned 9 yrs old and have not reached as far as we would like to see but there is always hope so we take it one day at a time.

Parents: Your children need you! Do not ever give up no matter how hard a struggle there is always some solution. We still go on each day fighting and searching for answers to the many burdens.

Martin

Sarah Jane May

Picture this: You're on a train. Along with you are several other people sitting quietly. However, a small family is also riding on it as well sitting across from you: two parents, a very quiet sister trying to avoid eye contact with you as much as possible pretending to be very interested on the map on the wall, and one very, very loud screaming/singing child rocking his head either side to side or back and forth. You stare at him. You are probably by now very uncomfortable. We, too, are uncomfortable.

It's not east being thirteen and having a cursing, loud, autistic child for a little brother. But you learn to deal with it. Sometimes. Other times, in front of your friends, he either curses or runs around. Now my friends learn to accept it and think its cute, but before, in the fourth grade, it was very tough.

This is why I hate the dreaded R word. Long before I knew there was a website to pledge never to say it, I had banned the words from my lips. That still didn't stop people from saying it. You can change one or two minds, but it is almost impossible to change a nation. People have asked me once before, "Is your brother Retarded?" to which they took the hint never to say again. It enrages me with anger and sadness because kids today have no idea what they are saying and what I can mean. To their peers it can mean an extremely funny joke, but to others, it can mean so much more. To me, it is like someone coming up to you and telling you that the religion you believe in is not real.

Many times I have wondered what my life would be like without Martin in my life. And I know the exact answer. Before Martin was diagnosed, both my mother and I never even knew any disorders or diseases. When I saw someone in a wheelchair, that was all that crossed my mind was that they has a physical disability. But it can be so much more. Whenever I saw a child screaming in a store or restaurant all I could think was "wow what a brat." Never to know that perhaps it was more than just the child acting up. Now because of my brother, I know when I see a child throwing a fit I don't think "brat". I think "sensory overload" or "schedule change" or something other than what most people think. And usually I just smile at the parent with understanding eyes because I know I've been there before.

I'm used to "The Stare". I've seen it way too much in the past Eight years to not be used to it. Once in a movie theatre, I was so upset over two people turning around in there seats to look at my brother that I yelled at them "What?!" and stared back with an angry expression. It makes me so upset to know that a large portion of the planet can't and never will know what it is like.

Not everything about Martin is negative. There's so much more to him than just his Asperger's. While he has his days, he can be so much fun. He's my best friend. He's also very protective and when anyone, including mom, scolds me he's always there to yell back at them, "Don't talk to her like that!" If only I could bring him to school with me.

He's very good to talk to. There are many people in our lives that are very kind and accepting. But there are people who have been very cruel and abusive to Martin. I don't know what his future will be like. I can only hope that he will know more when he is grown up.

I do not like self-contained classes in schools. I think it teaches children at an early age to fear children with autism or any other disorders. While many children now are kind and don't care if he is different, I know that most, in the future, will not be as accepting. Already now I have seen cruelty toward my brother by a bunch of eight-year-olds playing pranks on him. It is unfair and cruel, and children do not yet know how to make up their minds so adults make them up for them. This influence can be very negative for parents who don't understand. Then as the children get older, they turn into the people who don't understand and look at kids with disabilities like they are disgusting. This makes parents and siblings very upset.

I can only hope that society will change in the years to come.

Madison's Story

Michelle Broadnax

On December 21, 2001 a beautiful baby girl named Madison was born into the world. This precious baby brought such joy, love and laughter into our lives. I loved to just sit and watch her sleep, so peaceful, so angelic.

One day, soon after we brought Madison home from the hospital, I was watching her sleep and I noticed her body "twitching". Over the next few weeks, I noticed her "twitching" a couple more times. Already having an older child, I wasn't your typical paranoid new mother, but I did find myself quite concerned. I called the Pediatrician who said she was sure everything was fine and to just keep a watch on it. A couple of months later as Madison started scooting and sitting up, she started having "episodes" where she would stiffen up and rock back and forth, and would actually do this off and on all throughout the day.

We video taped these "episodes" and showed the Pediatrician exactly what Madison was doing. After viewing the videotapes, the Pediatrician started to get concerned as well, so she referred Madison to see a Neurologist. The Neurologist ran a bunch of tests, ordered an MRI and an EEG, but nothing abnormal was ever found. Since all of the tests appeared "normal", I thought maybe I was just overreacting. Madison's unexplained "episodes" continued for about a year and then when she finally started walking at 1 ½ years old the "episodes" just miraculously stopped.

I then began getting concerned that Madison seemed to be a little slower than other children her age, but when I would mention it to the Pediatrician I was told not to worry, that each child is different and everyone grows and learns differently and at their own pace. At that point I let it go and accepted the fact that Madison was just different and did things a little slower and differently than others.

It wasn't until Madison was 4 ½ years old and started Pre-K that her differences weren't just a concern of mine, but became of great concern to her teachers as well. Madison's Pre-K year was a very stressful year for us. On a daily basis I received calls from the school. We battled Madison saying she felt sick everyday, not wanting to go to school, crying all day, getting frustrated, and showing a great deal of anxiety with transitioning socially interacting with other children. At one point, I actually thought they were going to kick Madison out of Pre-K. All of her teachers were great and united together to come up with a plan to help Madison as much as they could. Madison's school encouraged me to talk to her Pediatrician again and to take along all of her school records and tests so she could see what all was going on and that there was more to it than me just being a "paranoid" Mom.

So, in June 2008 when Madison was 5 ½, I took her to meet with the Pediatrician to review all of her health records and school records and to discuss my concerns again. After going over everything for about an hour, the Pediatrician performed a few simple tests and then she told me she wanted Madison to see a couple of different specialists to confirm her feelings of what was going on with Madison.

That's when I first heard the word "autism". My emotions stood strong and I immediately started asking the Pediatrician all kinds of questions. What is autism? What causes it? What do I do? How did that happen? I had left the office not feeling good about any of the answers or should I say lack of answers that I had gotten.

We got to the car and I buckled Madison up in the back seat and then I got into the car and at that very moment, the word "autism" finally hit me. I broke down and cried. I pulled myself together and then called my husband and told him everything the Pediatrician had said and then we both sat on the phone and cried together.

After I got off the phone with my husband, I started the car to head home when out of nowhere Madison starts singing a song that she had just learned at vacation bible school, I looked at her in the rear view mirror and at that very moment she sang "Everything's Ok, Everything's Alright 'Cause I've got Jesus in My Life". I then realized that I had all the answers that I needed and that yes, everything was going to be all right because we do have Jesus in our life.

I then started my journey of putting the pieces of the puzzle together. In May of 2009, Madison was diagnosed with PDD-NOS. Although we have daily triumphs to overcome, Madison still brings

joy, love and laughter into our lives. And we are still working strong
on our journey to complete the puzzle.

Warm Fuzzies and Contentment
Teresa Johnson

Today, I feel so content. My oldest son has come home to visit through the weekend. It could be a while before he comes back. We will celebrate his 20th birthday with a steak dinner, a trip to the mall for some shopping, and a movie (Harry Potter's new one!). There is something wonderful about having him here. He is such fun, always laughing, telling funny stories or jokes, lighting up the atmosphere. He is growing up and I can't stand it! LOL!

My home is comfortable and the smell of pot roast is filling the entire house. In a few moments, dinner will be finished and my family of 4, complete, will sit down to an evening meal together. Our conversation will be full and thought provoking. Ryan will engage John and I at every turn with his thoughts about life, laws, school, you name it. And we will enjoy every minute of it.

Rusty loves it when his brother is here. They play games, watch movies together, shoot pool, hang out, just "be". Since they were small, Ryan has been the "supervisor" orchestrating everything to his liking, and Rusty, the loyal subject, following his every word to the letter. Ryan could pretty much convince Rusty to do anything. They have always been a fun pair to watch. Today is no different, the conversation is just more challenging for Rusty than when they were smaller.

So, I sit in my living room recliner, having finished up watching a movie with my boys, listening to Ryan's breathing as he sleeps. Rusty impatiently paces back and forth and up and down the stairs wanting to play pool, and his brother just sleeps. Peace. Contentment. Safety.

... and I have warm fuzzies of yesteryear and hoping for even better days ahead!

Magic
Shannon Johnson

This morning was very similar to yesterday morning. But it was nothing like the rest of the past 10 years. As I scramble around the kitchen throwing together breakfast and lunches for Steve and the kids, I find myself basking in the silence. Well, not exactly silence, but almost as close to silence as it gets around here. Haley is styling her hair and making her bed and Steve is helping Wynn in the shower.

The sounds coming from upstairs are more conversational than I can ever remember. Instead of the shrill reactions that have numbed me, my ears are witness to a daddy and his son bantering in the bathroom. I stop whizzing a smoothie and lean closer in. What I hear is nothing short of magic.

Can you help me rinse my hair?
Of course.
Can I dry myself off?

That would be great.

What's for breakfast, Dad?

I think mommy is making eggs.

Are you going to a meeting today?

Not today.

So I will see you after school?

Yep, you will.

Thanks, Dad.

You're welcome, bud.

My magic may not be magic to anyone else, but it is powerful enough to lift me high above......strong enough to wash away the fear that has ridden in my back pocket, taunting and haunting---bringing dread into my throat. Fanciful enough to sprinkle my imagination with a future that includes health and sanity and a complete family unit....In a blink, all is well. That kind of magic......

We eat a quick breakfast together. In the air is the buzz of a morning full of deadlines and buses to catch, bills to pay and tread mills to conquer....In a rhythm that is almost like a dance, we grab backpacks and lunchboxes, keys and wallets and step into the new day.

I look back at my husband before I close the garage door. In his eyes I notice a twinkle......a little bit of hope for tomorrow...a little bit of magic for the day.

Independence

Margaret Spielman

We are at Myrtle Beach this week on vacation.

I thought that this would be another one of those trips where my family would get to spend time in the sand and waves and I would spend time in the room with Hunter. He has always been terrified of water and would rather "get a room" than anything else. Vacations for me have been ok but it has always been a struggle trying to balance it with the other kids. I remember thinking, as I watched moms from the balcony reading their books and sunbathing while their children were in the pool playing, that I would never be able to experience that.

For those of you with older children you know what I am talking about. The age when finally you can relax and watch your child play in the pool or spend the night off at a friend's house: The age of independence. Since his cognitive age is 3, independence is not something that Hunter is able to achieve to the degree of a typical 13 year old.

I am happy to report that he actually got in the ocean today - the first time EVER he has done this. He let the waves knock him down, he let his feet be buried in the sand and we built a small but respectable sand castle. He also found that he loves the pool. We stayed outside for five hours. He is already talking about getting up early and going to the beach to build a castle. The beast is unleashed!

I often find myself wanting just to be a normal mom with normal problems but then I look at all the wonderful adventures Hunter takes me on. I realize that although my life is anything but normal it is full of honesty, fun and most of all love. I need him as much as he needs me.

One of my favorite quotes is "Hope is not the closing your eyes to the difficulty or the risk or the failure. It is a trust that....if I fail now....I shall not fail forever and if I am hurt, I shall be healed. It is a trust that life is good, love is powerful, and the future is full of promise." Hunter gives me the hope and courage to face life, to fail, to win but most of all, to love.

This is just one more mountain we have climbed and the view from the top is amazing!

Augie's Autism: A Journey to Recovery
Georgia Fruechtenicht

Augie was almost three when he pulled a lamp off a desk onto himself. The light bulb burned a perfect circle into his knee. I picked up my screaming child and could smell the burnt flesh. I enjoyed holding him in the rocker, even though he was crying loudly. If he was awake, Augie was usually too busy to sit in my lap. My friends referred to him as "all boy," but I wondered if there was more to it. A minute of comforting was all it took before Augie was back up on his tip toes prancing around the room babbling in a language that only he understood. A band-aid was out of the question. He would not let anything sticky touch his skin. Ten minutes later, Augie was happily crawling on his knees on the carpet, his burned knee alternating evenly with the non-burned one. He didn't even flinch or seem to notice the missing layers of skin on his bloody knee. It was at that moment that I realized that something was terribly wrong with my son. I could justify the lack of language: boys talk later than girls; all children develop at different rates. I could justify the lack of social skills: when he develops language, the social skills will come. I could justify the strange behaviors: he's kind of weird like his daddy. I had no justification, however, for why he didn't seem to feel pain.

The week before, he had played with the knobs in the bathtub and had turned the water to all hot. I returned from checking on his sister, Virginia, to find him sitting in a tub full of boiling hot water. He was as pink as a boiled shrimp, with wet hair and sweat running down his flushed face. He was happily counting his ducks. One to ten, then ten to one, then back to ten....

The pediatrician said, "He's a tough kid." About the constant diarrhea, he said, "Some kids just don't poop solid." About the lack of language, he said, "He'll talk when he's ready." Augie recognized all his alphabet letters, could read a few words, could count to 50, and could even say the alphabet backwards. But he still did not say "Mommy." I didn't want to "wait and see" any longer. He told me about Babies Can't Wait and gave me a referral to a Developmental Pediatrician. Then, as I left his office, he patted me on the back and said, "Relax, you worry too much. He'll be fine."

The Babies Can't Wait evaluation showed that Augie, who was almost three, had the overall language of a nine month old. His language was two full years delayed. They also saw "red flags for autism" and "sensory integration dysfunction." I was not familiar with either term. I now cringe at my ignorance and denial. My only question for the evaluators was "is he going to die from this?"

The word "autism" was not one I was ready to deal with. In an effort to keep from shutting down with anxiety and depression, I chose to focus on Sensory Integration Dysfunction, now known as Sensory Processing Disorder. I was fascinated. I finally understood why Augie loved to crash into things. Why he walked on his tiptoes. I understood his holding his hands over his ears and spinning. I understood the staring at his hands as if they weren't connected to his body, and his inability to point to his own body parts. I knew why he stuffed way too much food in his mouth. I even knew why he didn't feel pain. I now understood his obsessive need to line things up. He was trying to find a way to cope with a world that was extremely confusing to him.

A friend suggested that I find a clinic that does "intensives," which means several therapy appointments every day for several weeks. Two weeks later, we began therapy at a clinic in Winterpark, Florida called LifeSkills. Augie had two hours of Occupational Therapy and an hour and a half of Speech Therapy each day. It was exhausting, but the results were worth it. The starting gun of Augie's development fired, and Augie took off sprinting. On Day Three of the intensive, Augie started singing songs. He sang the "ABC Song" first, of course, and then "Baa Baa Black Sheep." Over the next few days, he added "Twinkle Twinkle Little Star," and "Jesus Loves Me." On Day Four, he came running into the kitchen where I was cooking dinner, looked me in the eye, and said "Mommy, I …." and then babbled a complete paragraph that I did not understand. Even though I had no idea what he was telling me, he had called me by name and he connected with me to tell me about something that interested him. He had never said my name to get my attention.

During Week Two, he began to make a choice between two things. I had been working on this for months. I'd ask, "Augie want milk or juice?" and hold up both. He'd either look at me like he was confused or just repeat "Augie want milk or juice?" Now, he had an opinion, even expressed it without being asked, "Augie want milk!"

I was overwhelmed with hopefulness and optimism about his future. I wrote lengthy letters to my in laws explaining what I was learning and documenting Augie's progress. I was also completely drained at the end of the two weeks. When my husband Gary showed up to drive us home, I collapsed into him.

After returning to South Georgia, Augie had an appointment with a Developmental Pediatrician. She diagnosed him with Pervasive Developmental Disorder-Not Otherwise Specified (PDD-NOS) after a one-hour evaluation. She explained that PDD-NOS is one of the Autism Spectrum Disorders, and that there is no cure. She recommended starting an intense behavioral intervention program (ABA). She said it was too early to tell if Augie would ever function in mainstream society, but with intense intervention, he "might do just fine." She warned us not to "Google" Autism on the Internet because it would just scare us. And she warned us of the "crazy expensive diets that don't work."

After reading Children with Starving Brains, by Jacqueline McCandes, I was anxious to start biomedical treatment. I had been warned about the long waiting list to see Dr. Nathanson-Lippitt, a "DAN!" doctor in Atlanta, but my research told me that she was the doctor we needed. I was crushed when her office told me that it would be one year before Augie could get an evaluation. I put Augie's name on the cancellation list and prayed for the phone to ring. I packed a bag and kept it in the closet in case her office called. Once a week, I called and "touched base." Even without an appointment with a DAN! doctor, I knew that we needed to start some dietary interventions, and some basic supplements (a multivitamin, some omega 3 fatty acids, and a probiotic). Two weeks after eliminating ALL milk (casein) from Augie's diet, his skin was as clear as porcelain. He looked pale without the red eczema splotches on his cheeks. He no longer itched. He no longer needed the big tub of cortisone. His nose stopped running. He also stopped beating his head on the wall, and he stopped screaming. Six weeks later, Augie began to ask questions. He was three and a half. We were in the car driving home from preschool, and Augie asked "Daddy lunch?" He wanted to know if his Daddy was coming home for lunch. He was also suddenly interested in Virginia, and actually concerned for her safety. He ran into the bathroom and yelled "Uh Oh Mommy! Jija! Uh Oh!" I went into the living room to find Virginia stuck under the couch and crying. Two months before, Augie would have responded to Virginia's crying by putting his hands over his ears, spinning, and crying himself.

Dr. Nathanson-Lippitt's office called three months later. In order to prepare, I called Augie's church preschool teacher to get her feedback to share with the doctor. She had been very positive about how much Augie had improved since we gave up milk. I asked her to "tell me about Augie's interaction with other children." Her answer shocked me. She said "Augie does not interact with other children, but he stands a little closer than he used to. And he watches them."

I was upset, "But you've been telling me he's doing great in school. I thought he was improving."

She said, "He is improving. He doesn't scream as much. And he watches the other kids. He talks to me some now, but he still doesn't talk to the other kids."

Dr. Nathanson-Lippitt confirmed the diagnosis of PDD-NOS and then added a few more: "Developmental Language Disorder,

Obsessive Compulsive Ideation, and Sensory Integrative Dysfunction." After receiving the lab work, she added "Chronic Intestinal Dysbiosis, Heavy Metal Encephalopathy, and Metabolic Disorder." The difference in this doctor and the first developmental pediatrician was considerable. Her first words to us were "We've got work to do." She spent over an hour explaining the results of her two-hour evaluation. She was pleased with Augie's progress since the Babies Can't Wait Evaluation. According to her testing, Augie's overall language scored an age equivalent of one year, eleven months (he was three years, six months). It was still an eighteen-month delay, which is certainly significant, but it was an encouraging improvement from the two-year delay we had just six months earlier. Dr. Nathanson-Lippitt felt strongly that we needed to go ahead and remove gluten from Augie's diet. She ordered an IGG Food Sensitivity Test, which showed severe sensitivities to gluten, eggs, soy, and milk. We left her office with a stapled stack of resources and a list of things we needed to do for Augie in the four weeks before our next appointment. We were overwhelmed, exhausted, and scared, but hopeful and encouraged that there was a course of treatment available.

Behaviorally, Augie regressed after giving up gluten. He became wilder with even less body awareness than before. He was screaming again, crashing into people, walls, and furniture. His diarrhea, which had improved, became worse. I was scared, even though I knew from my research that regression was a good sign.

After about a week, he woke up and the psychotic look in his eyes was gone. I asked him simple questions and he heard me, and answered with words or gestures. He started eating better. We had also added supplements of zinc, calcium and magnesium.

Treating his zinc deficiency helped him feel hungry. His teacher called me at home to tell me that he played a whole game of Ring Around The Rosie with some girls in class. And that he had to sit in time out for throwing a rock at a kid. I was thrilled that he was aware of the kid. She had never before been pleased to report to a parent that a child had been to time out. Three weeks after we removed gluten, I walked Augie into the church for preschool. He responded to the pastor's "Good Morning, Augie," with his own "Good Morning." He looked him in the eye instead of looking at the ground as he had done for two years. When we got to his class, he walked up to a little boy he had known for two years. He asked, "Andrew? Play trains?"

I held my breath in anticipation of Andrew's response. Andrew and Augie met eyes and smiled at each other, and then ran over to the train table to play trains. I doubted immediately if it had really happened. The tears in his teacher's eyes confirmed that it had. He was connecting with his peers.

Unfortunately, all of his social advances weren't as graceful. Suddenly, he was outgoing and wanting to connect with his peers, but he did not know how. One day, Gary, Augie, and I were at a park when Augie walked up to every kid on the playground and said "Hi, my name Augie. A-U-G-I-E spell 'Augie.'" Then he would stare at the kid, shrug his shoulders, and walk off. Most of the kids were older and looked at him like he was crazy. One little girl looked at him unsurely, and said, "My name is Madeline." Augie just looked at her, shrugged his shoulders and walked off. Gary tried to help him out, and encouraged him to ask, "What is your name?" to the next child. It was obvious he was not going to be done with this exercise until he spoke to every child at the crowded playground.

He walked up to another little boy, and said, "Hi, my name Augie, A-U-G-I-E spell 'Augie.' What you name?" The little boy said, "Fisher." Augie stared at him, shrugged his shoulders, and walked off. One kid got a special introduction. It was "Hi, my name Augie, A-U-G-I-E spell 'Augie.' Last name, Femdick, F-R-U-E-C-H-T-E-N-I-C-H-T spell Femdick. What you name?" Gary and I cringed, and then encouraged him to leave "Fruechtenicht" out of his introductions until he was a little older.

Treating the intestinal yeast involved a similar regression to the one Augie had when we eliminated gluten, only this one was accompanied by intense, bright yellow, stringy, and unpredictable diarrhea, and projectile throw ups. He spent long periods of time lining up cars and putting alphabet letters into order. His eczema came back and he scratched himself until he bled.

Then, after six days, a curtain lifted and Augie jumped out and said, clear as a bell, "WATCH THIS, MOMMY!" and "MOMMY, VAGIGA (Virginia), WAIT FOR ME!" His spontaneous language exploded! He could talk in complete sentences and have simple conversations. He noticed things and commented on his observations. One night, Gary walked in the house from work, and Augie volunteered, "Hey Daddy! Vagiga's sleeping. Mommy's cooking dinner. And I've got a sucker! See?"

At our next visit to Dr. Nathanson-Lippitt, she told us that he was healthy enough for chelation. Augie's initial tests showed a significant body burden of heavy metals and an inability to detox appropriately. We had to correct some severe nutritional deficiencies and treat his yeast before she would consider chelation. The chelation process was difficult, with regression in days two through six of each cycle, but the improvement was dramatic in all areas. Augie went from being socially awkward to being able to make friends. He started gaining weight, eating a wider variety of food, and asking more questions. He started making jokes and understanding sarcasm. He no longer acted like a child with Autism.

On December 11, 2007, almost two months after Augie's fifth birthday, Dr. Nathanson-Lippitt told Gary and me that she no longer considered Augie to be a child on the Autism Spectrum. She said, "He's still quirky as hell, but he's definitely not autistic." I knew that Augie wasn't autistic anymore, but hearing the words come from her mouth was special and I'll remember it always.

Augie had a psychological evaluation with the school several months later. He did not qualify for services under Autism. He no longer had a language disorder because his testing with the speech therapist showed his language was at age level. They found no evidence of a learning disability, ADD, or ADHD. He qualified for consultative services based on teacher observations.

Augie had a remarkable kindergarten year with an amazing teacher who loved to move and expected greatness from ALL of her students. Augie thrived in her class, although his literal thinking made it confusing at times. One day, he got in the car and said "Bad news, Mom. Mrs. Tarleton told me I need to worry about myself...(pause)....but I don't know what to worry about."

He got furious that I laughed at him and told me through tears that I hurt his feelings. He was genuinely confused by her comment. Another time, Mrs. Tarleton told the class to write a report on "what you want to be when you grow up." Augie wrote his report on "being a beaver." When Mrs. Tarleton called him up to her desk, she explained that he was supposed to write the report on *a job*. He was surprised, and said "OH, you didn't say what JOB I want to be. I want to be a zoo keeper. I'll write about that."

Augie is in first grade now. His reading and math skills are above grade level, and his conduct grade is 100%. His teacher says that he is a leader in the class, and he has a gift of helping the struggling learners. He has a group of boys who are his friends and one who is his "best friend." He loves riding the bus home and introduced us to many of his "bus friends" at the Fall Festival. One of his bus friends is a little girl named Hannah Grace, a kindergartener who affectionately calls him "Boppy Head." Augie announced at dinner one night that he's going to marry her because he loves her. He quotes her as an authority on all subjects and generally works her name into conversation whenever he can. He obviously has a huge crush on her, although he doesn't know that's what it's called.

Today, when I tell people that Augie was diagnosed with Autism when he was three, the responses vary. Some simply don't believe me. Some assume that he was misdiagnosed because "there's no cure for Autism." My favorite response is "so you really can *grow out* of Autism." Some say, "It must have been a mild case..."

But, the moms of children with Autism Spectrum Disorders want answers. They ask the question "Which therapy worked?" The answer is not that simple. Augie's recovery was a combination of many interventions coming together. Diet and supplementation played a big role in healing his gut and brain, but it also wouldn't have happened without treating the yeast and getting the metals out. Sensory Integration therapy, both with an OT and at home, was important to get his brain stem to correctly interpret information. Augie also is a very intelligent kid, and I think that improved his response to treatment. Having committed parents, who were willing to spend much of their time and available resources, including some retirement savings, and do the exhausting work of coordinating it all, was also a contributing factor. It's a complex puzzle that is still coming together. While the autism is gone, some sensory processing and gut issues remain. But you certainly won't hear us complaining. Augie's recovery is a gift from God. A precious gift that Gary and I will never take for granted.

I Can't Do It

Polly Bouker

If I had a dollar for every time someone told me what a great job I do parenting my son and that he or she "couldn't do it", I would surely be rich.

Are the parents of special needs children any better prepared to care for our children? Are we born with a special set of skills? No. At least I wasn't. As a matter of fact, there are many days when "I can't do it" either.

Whether or not we "do it" isn't determined by our abilities. It is determined by the fact that we are parents and we love our kids. Our children have needs that we must handle. If we don't help them, nobody will.

I don't enjoy the tantrums, the hitting, spitting, or biting. I didn't go to college to learn how to use various psychological techniques to target dangerous behaviors. I didn't apply for this position to work with special needs individuals. Instead, I decided to be a mother, and with that came the responsibility to help my child when others will not.

As a parent of a special needs child, I don't want the admiration or compliments from others. I want people to realize that they could "do it" if their child needed them to do so.

The Race We Run

Cheryl Killman

Un-describable, the joy that we felt
With a thankful heart, to God we knelt.
Our baby, our child, our love, such joy.
God blessed us with a beautiful baby boy.

We marveled at your inquisitive eyes
Felt so proud at five months when you learned "bye bye"
We laughed, we played and made silly faces
You learned to crawl, then to walk.........too many places.

We thought we were doing all that we could
We got your vaccinations like the Doctors said we should
Please forgive us Son, how were we to know the reasons
That your little body could not handle all the poisons

Then like a thief slips in during the night of your home
Our happy little baby boy was suddenly ....gone
No playing, no pee-pie, no more talking did you do

You ignored me like one deaf as I talked to you

Gone were the smiles, the hugs and the sparkle in your eyes
The Dr. said Autism, I did not want to believe such lies.
Look at me, Look at me, Kile if you can.
Please come back to me, please hold my hand.

I love you, I love you, my heart, my son.
Autism is treatable, this marathon we will run
The hours, the research, the tears, the cost
I want my little boy back, I will not let him be lost.

So Kile, as others look at you with staring eyes
When you talk to your fingers, and tell them goodbye
Please know baby, mommy is setting the pace
Together, one mile at a time, we will win this race.

Someday you will play ball and ride a bike
And hang out with daddy on a 10 mile hike
We'll go to Disney World and see Mickey Mouse
And remove all the chains and locks in your house.

Someday you'll get your very own boat
As a family down the Natty River we will float.
You'll laugh, you'll talk, you'll sing us a song
Because Jesus is a healer and the doctors were wrong.

As we place the pieces of this puzzle together
And unravel the mystery of Autism forever
I hope you will always know my son,
You are the reason for the race we run.

To my son, Kile
My reason, my heart.

Acknowledgements

Thank you to all of the contributors and their loved ones for sharing their stories and offering a glimpse into their world.

Polly Bouker & Teresa Johnson

Rusty

Jon

Made in the USA
Charleston, SC
25 November 2009